Residential and Service-population Exposure to Multiple Natural Hazards in the Mount Hood Region of Clackamas County, Oregon

By Amy M. Mathie and Nathan Wood

Prepared in cooperation with the Clackamas County Emergency Management Department

Open-File Report 2013–1073

U.S. Department of the Interior
U.S. Geological Survey

U.S. Department of the Interior
SALLY JEWELL, Secretary

U.S. Geological Survey
Suzette M. Kimball, Acting Director

U.S. Geological Survey, Reston, Virginia: 2013

For more information on the USGS—the Federal source for science about the Earth,
its natural and living resources, natural hazards, and the environment—visit
http://www.usgs.gov or call 1–888–ASK–USGS

For an overview of USGS information products, including maps, imagery, and publications,
visit *http://www.usgs.gov/pubprod*

Suggested citation:
Mathie, A.M., and Wood, N., 2013, Residential and service-population exposure to multiple natural hazards in the
Mount Hood region of Clackamas County, Oregon: U.S. Geological Survey Open-File Report 2013–1073, available at
http://pubs. usgs.gov/of/2013/1073/ .

Any use of trade, product, or firm names is for descriptive purposes only and does not imply
endorsement by the U.S. Government.

Contents

Figures

Tables

Residential and Service-population Exposure to Multiple Natural Hazards in the Mount Hood Region of Clackamas County, Oregon

By Amy M. Mathie and Nathan Wood

Abstract

The objective of this research is to document residential and service-population exposure to natural hazards in the rural communities of Clackamas County, Oregon, near Mount Hood. The Mount Hood region of Clackamas County has a long history of natural events that have impacted its small, tourism-based communities. To support preparedness and emergency-management planning in the region, a geospatial analysis of population exposure was used to determine the number and type of residents and service populations in flood-, wildfire-, and volcano-related hazard zones. Service populations are a mix of residents and tourists temporarily benefitting from local services, such as retail, education, or recreation. In this study, service population includes day-use visitors at recreational sites, overnight visitors at hotels and resorts, children at schools, and community-center visitors. Although the heavily-forested, rural landscape suggests few people are in the area, there are seasonal peaks of thousands of visitors to the region. "Intelligent" dasymetric mapping efforts using 30-meter resolution land-cover imagery and U.S. Census Bureau data proved ineffective at adequately capturing either the spatial distribution or magnitude of population at risk. Consequently, an address-point-based hybrid dasymetric methodology of assigning population to the physical location of buildings mapped with a global positioning system was employed. The resulting maps of the population (1) provide more precise spatial distributions for hazard-vulnerability assessments, (2) depict appropriate clustering due to higher density structures, such as apartment complexes and multi-unit commercial buildings, and (3) provide new information on the spatial distribution and temporal variation of people utilizing services within the study area.

Estimates of population exposure to flooding, wildfire, and volcanic hazards were determined by using overlay analysis in a geographic information system. Population exposure to flood hazards is low (less than 10 percent of residents) and does not vary substantially between 100-year and 500-year flood-hazard scenarios. Moderate, moderate-to-high, and high wildfire-risk areas within the study region account for 72 percent of residents, 62 percent of employees, and 60 percent of daytime visitors to recreation sites. Fifteen percent of businesses in the study area are in moderate-to-high or high wildfire-risk areas but these businesses represent 51 percent of the local workforce. A volcanic event at Mount Hood could directly impact up to 60 percent of residents in their homes and 87 percent of employees at their workplaces. The proximal volcanic-hazard zone alone includes 65 percent of employees, 80 percent of schools and community facilities, more than 60 percent of overnight visitors in peak seasons, and 82–100 percent of daytime visitors to recreation sites during the summer and winter months, respectively. The number of day-use visitors to recreation sites in the region is greatest during winter months (averaging 129,300 people per month), whereas overnight visitors are greatest during summer months (averaging 34,000 per month). This analysis of residential and service-population exposure to natural hazards supports the development of targeted risk-reduction efforts in the region, while also expanding the discourse on characterizing and assessing population dynamics in tourist-frequented areas.

Introduction

Societal risk to natural hazards is a function of human development in areas prone to such physical events. To effectively manage these risks, public officials need to gauge the potential for future events (the hazards) and the exposure, sensitivity, and adaptive capacity (collectively referred to as vulnerability) of systems relative to the perceived hazards (Wood, 2011). Systems of interest typically include populations, economic assets and regional economies, critical facilities and infrastructure, and ecosystems. Understanding the vulnerability of these systems to natural hazards enables emergency managers, public officials, business owners, and the general public to make informed decisions about how they may want to mitigate, prepare for, respond to, and recover from the potential consequences of future events. This report describes the exposure of residential and service populations to flood, wildfire, and volcano hazards within the Villages at Mount Hood and Government Camp region of Clackamas County, Oreg., and results from collaboration between the Clackamas County Department of Emergency Management and the U.S. Geological Survey.

Population vulnerability to natural hazards often is characterized using data compiled in national population counts. In the United States, the U.S. Census Bureau provides decadal counts and annual estimates of the number and demographic characteristics of the residential population (U.S. Census Bureau, 2012). Residential population of an area is based upon an individual's residence and not by the geographic area an individual typically occupies (for example, workplace, recreation sites, and markets). Because of privacy concerns, census counts do not reflect individual residences and instead are provided in aggregated areal units (for example census blocks, block groups, and tracts) that generalize population distribution across the landscape. Although useful for hazards that cover large geographic areas (for example, earthquakes and hurricanes), the aggregated areal units have limited utility for other hazards that have relatively small footprints, such as floods or volcanic lahars. This is particularly an issue in rural areas where census blocks (the smallest census unit) can be large and may be larger than hazard zones.

Another limitation of relying only on census counts for population-exposure assessments is that various types of visitors (collectively called a service population) can outnumber residents in many areas but are not accounted for in census counts. Service populations are defined as the people, either residents or tourists, who temporarily enter an area to receive some sort of service or benefit, such as transportation access (commuters), recreation (day-use and overnight tourists), goods (shoppers at a market), or education (school children) (Cook, 1996; Australian Bureau of Statistics, 2008). Service populations are neither discrete nor mutually exclusive and individuals can belong to multiple segments (Australian Bureau of Statistics, 2008). For example, a family may live, work, shop, recreate, and send children to local daycare at various points within the study area. If individuals are permanent residents, U.S. Census Bureau counts will include them at their point of residence (aggregated into a generalized census unit), but will not indicate the other areas commonly frequented. If the family only lives in the area during a peak tourist season, their presence and use of services in the region is unlikely to be recorded at all. The value of recognizing a service-population component is illustrated in a study of population exposure to tsunami hazards on the Oregon coast, where Wood and Good (2004) estimated that non-residents (for example, commuting employees and tourists) comprised more than two-thirds of the at-risk population in two coastal communities. Emergency managers and public officials need better methods for assessing residential and service-population exposure to hazards if they are to develop realistic mitigation, preparedness, response, and recovery strategies.

One area with a wide array of natural hazards, rural development, and substantial service populations is the upper Sandy River valley and Mount Hood region of Clackamas County, Oregon (fig. 1). The rural residential development and recreational opportunities of this region largely center around a primary transportation corridor (U.S. Highway 26) that runs through multiple hazard zones associated with volcanic, flood, landslide, and wildfire hazards. Some of the hazards, such as those related to volcanic activity, can be highly unpredictable in terms of their speed of onset and event duration, which creates significant emergency management and land-use challenges for public officials who are attempting to balance public safety, quality of life and livelihoods, and economic development. Although there have been several studies to assess the natural hazards in this area, less has been done to understand the vulnerability of communities to these hazards (for instance, Burns and others, 2011), and no attention has been paid to service populations.

To better understand population dynamics and hazard exposure in this area, the Clackamas County Emergency Management Department sought assistance from the U.S. Geological Survey (USGS) to (1) determine the number, type, and temporal trends in residential and service populations and (2) determine the exposure of these populations to a variety of natural hazards in the area. This information helps public safety officials and community planners to understand where and when people are concentrated in hazardous areas for the sake of emergency notification, evacuation planning, limiting or restricting access, and estimating losses to economic productivity. This information enables emergency managers to develop targeted outreach and preparedness plans that address local needs and issues. It also provides a foundation for efficient and effective plans for emergency response and recovery.

Purpose and Scope

The objective of this report is to document residential and service-population exposure to natural hazards in the rural communities of Clackamas County, Oregon, near Mount Hood. The various population data sources and population-modeling techniques used to estimate population distributions across space and time are discussed in this report. Seasonal variations are estimated for tourism-related businesses and locations. Hazard exposure is based on the number of people and locations (for example, trailheads and businesses) in published flood, wildfire, and volcano hazard zones. These hazards were chosen as a result of county interest and data availability for the study area. Additional natural hazards common in the study area include landslides and severe winter storms (Clackamas County, Oregon, 2007); however, population-exposure estimates were not possible for these hazards because spatially-explicit data on hazard susceptibility were insufficient or nonexistent.

Population-exposure estimates should not be construed as loss estimates for a future extreme event because of the unpredictable nature of future events and because of the dynamic nature of population magnitudes and distributions. For example, a volcanic eruption is expected to be preceded by a period of unrest that will be monitored, which should provide opportunities to protect people and property. Similar pre-event opportunities for monitoring and evacuation are likely before extreme flood or wildfire conditions emerge. Population estimates are not intended to represent the number of people at a specific location as an event occurs because warnings, evacuations, or other emergency-management efforts likely will have occurred. These estimates do, however, indicate the magnitude and variability of people requiring consideration for success of such emergency plans. This work is intended

3

to support local, county, and State emergency managers directly in their efforts to develop realistic and effective outreach efforts, plans, and policies. For those outside of the study area, this research will help other emergency and land-use managers to become better aware of the dynamic nature of populations and of how service-population exposure to various natural hazards is a relevant factor for emergency-management planning.

Study Area

Clackamas County is located in northwest Oregon and is one of three counties that comprise the Portland, Oreg., metropolitan area (fig. 1A). With more than 400,000 residents, it is the third most populous county in the State (Oregon Blue Book, 2012) and has consistently shown population growth in recent decades which is projected to continue (Clackamas County, Oregon, 2002). The landscape is dominated by the Mount Hood volcano (within the Mount Hood National Forest) on the northeastern border of the county (fig. 1B and C). The county is largely forested and has numerous rivers and watersheds (for example, Bull Run, Sandy, Salmon, and Clackamas). Agriculture and urban development is concentrated in the western part of the county. The county's economy has long relied on agriculture, timber harvesting, manufacturing, and tourism (Clackamas County, Oregon, 2012), all of which are supported by access to nearby U.S. Interstate Highways (5, 205, and 84) and U.S. Highway 26, which runs west-east across the county.

This study focuses on the unincorporated communities along U.S. Highway 26 east of the City of Sandy to its connection with Oregon State Highway 35 at the southern base of Mount Hood (fig. 1C). This includes the community of Government Camp and the Villages at Mount Hood (VMH), which represents the communities of Brightwood, Wemme, Welches, Zigzag, and Rhododendron. The study area is delineated by the collective extents of seven 2010 U.S. Census Bureau block groups that include these unincorporated communities (U.S. Census Bureau, 2012)[1].

The VMH are part of a nationally recognized, citizen-driven "Hamlets and Villages" program in which unincorporated communities are governed by a locally elected board of directors and are provided staff liaisons and a small operating budget by the county (Clackamas County, Oregon, 2012). Although actions related to natural hazards may be taken locally (for example, home evaluations of wildfire susceptibility made by Hoodland Fire District), emergency planning and response coordination are performed at the county level for these unincorporated towns (Clackamas County, Oregon, 2012). The study area lacks hospitals or emergency rooms but has four schools, including three public schools of the Oregon Trail School District (Welches Elementary, Firwood Elementary, and Welches Middle School) and one private, sport-related school (Mount Hood Academy). There is also a community center located in Welches that houses a senior center and two separate childcare facilities.

Based on 2001 land-cover data, the majority of the study area is classified as forest (78 percent by area) followed distantly by grassland or shrub (15 percent), agricultural land (3 percent) and developed land (less than one percent) (fig. 2). Land cover percentages were derived from the 2001 National Land Cover Database (NLCD) (Homer and others, 2007), which is generated by automated techniques from 30-meter spatial resolution Landsat Enhanced Thematic Mapper Plus digital satellite imagery and verified with field visits (Homer and others, 2007; Loveland and Shaw, 1996). NLCD data

---

[1]This differs from the study area used by Burns and others (2011) which included the full extent of the Sandy River in Clackamas and Multnomah Counties, as well as the Hood River Valley in Hood River County to the north-east of Mount Hood. Results by Burns and others (2011) aggregate populations across the entire study area, therefore, caution should be taken in comparing results between the two studies.

include four types of developed classes (open space, low intensity, medium intensity, and high intensity) to reflect the level of impervious surfaces in a grid cell (for example, parking lots and roofs). The open-space developed classification is reported separately from the others because it primarily identifies areas of managed vegetation (for example parks, private yards) and not structures. For those not familiar with data derived from satellite imagery, it is important to note that the developed classes denote the amount of impervious surfaces within a grid cell (gauged by reflectance values in satellite data) and not the density of development (for example, "high-intensity" developed is not the same as high-density developed).

The study area includes the upper region of the Sandy River basin—an area that commonly experiences flooding. The Sandy River is a tributary to the Columbia River, which is the largest river in the Pacific Northwest region and serves as much of the border between Oregon and Washington State (Taylor, 1998). The Sandy River originates on the steep slopes of Mount Hood and drops more than 3,000 feet in elevation in 56 miles (approximately 90 kilometers)—the vast majority of the elevation loss, however, occurs before the confluence of the Sandy River with the Salmon River in the VMH area (Pierson and others, 2011). Consequently, the river channels within this section of the watershed can flow fast in floods and swiftly funnel lahars derived from Mount Hood volcanic unrest.

The study area provides a wide range of year-round recreational activities and settings (fig. 3). The winter season is dominated by snow sports (for example, snowboarding and alpine and cross-country skiing), and the summer season has a wide range of activities, such as climbing, hiking, and camping on U.S. Forest Service land, resort-style golfing, fishing, lake and river sports, and ski and snowboard camps on Mount Hood's Palmer snowfield. Fall and spring are less busy but still attract visitors, as well as school nature programs. Easy access along Highway 26 and close proximity to the Portland metropolitan area (approximately 1–2 hours) make this region a significant tourist draw, especially on holidays and weekends. To capitalize on these recreational opportunities, an urban renewal project was approved in 1989 by Clackamas County to encourage development of retail businesses, restaurants, overnight accommodations, and recreational facilities (Clackamas County, Oregon, 2012). To date, this tourism-driven development has occurred largely in the communities of Government Camp and Welches.

Population Distributions

To estimate population exposure to natural hazards in the study area, geographic-information-system (GIS) tools were used to integrate publicly available hazard and socioeconomic data, as well as population data developed specifically for this research. Unlike other population-modeling work done for the Mount Hood region (for example, Burns and others, 2011), this study does not limit population to permanent residents but focuses on residential and service populations, including residents in homes, employees at their workplace, overnight visitors (lodgers), daytime visitors to recreation sites, and dependents (children and seniors) at schools and community facilities. There are sure to be overlaps among the population groups (for example, residents that work at a local business and hike on a nearby trail); therefore, estimates for each group should not be added to estimate total population in the study area. The following sections describe how each population was mapped and how their sizes were estimated.

Population Locations

The first step in assessing population exposure to various natural hazards is to locate people on the landscape properly. Populations related to outdoor places (for example, trailheads and campgrounds entrances) were located using point data provided by the U.S. Forest Service. These data depict entrances to outdoor areas but do not delineate the full linear (in the case of trails) or areal (in the case of campgrounds) extent; therefore, care should be taken when interpreting results. Delineating campground extents and trail paths would improve the understanding of population distributions at these sites, but was considered beyond the scope of the current project.

Populations related to indoor places (for example, homes and businesses) were located using point data of building locations in a 2009 Master Street Address (MSA) file provided by Clackamas County. These data were developed using global positioning system (GPS) field equipment as part of a county wildfire prevention program. The original data simply identified address locations as GIS vector points and did not have additional information on building outlines (also known as footprints), type, use, or ownership. Tax-parcel data (2009 version) were used as ancillary information to expand the attributes of the MSA file but were not used directly in the GIS-based exposure analyses owing to known alignment issues between parcel data and other imagery and population data. This alignment issue existed because the county, until quite recently, lacked adequate survey-control data in various parts of the study area that is necessary to remap the parcels (Kelly Neumeier, Clackamas County Technology Services, Geographic Information Systems Division, written commun., 2012). Until this alignment issue was resolved, any exposure analysis based on existing parcel data likely will contain errors.

Population locations from the U.S. Forest Service and MSA data were classified into several building types, including residential homes, vacation homes, lodging accommodations, commercial businesses and industry, and recreational sites. This classification was based on several different sources, including 2009 tax parcels (Clackamas County Tax Assessor, unpub. data, 2009), 2009 Employer Database (InfoGroup, 2009), visual interpretation of imagery (National Agriculture Imagery Program, 2005), field verification, and private vacation-home locations (U.S. Forest Service, oral commun., 2011).

One issue encountered during the classification process was the inconsistent nature in which multiple businesses or homes within one structure were handled in the MSA data. For example, one strip mall comprised of several businesses would be described by one MSA point in some cases and as individual points in other cases. While a "yes - no" notation in the MSA data reflected the presence of a multi-unit building, there was not always additional descriptive information (for example, residential complex, multi-unit commercial facility, or mixed-use facility). This issue arose with certain retail centers, apartment and townhome complexes, condominium buildings, and large hotels and resorts. Many of the resorts (Collins Lake Resort, Whispering Woods Resort, and The Resort at the Mountain) had each rental unit marked as a distinct point but others (Shadowhawk Condos and Timberline Lodge) were summarized as single points. Although mapping large resorts by unit happened to be beneficial for this study (namely, when comparing population at spatially expansive facilities against spatially specific hazard zones), the additional feature points do tend to suggest more overnight lodging and day-use recreation sites than actually exist according to business license. Effort was made to be consistent with this issue; however, some inconsistencies remain.

Figure 4 depicts a final population-location database summarizing the updated MSA residential and business data and data for U.S. Forest Service outdoor locations. This report recognizes three classes of structures: (1) residence, (2) commercial or industrial business, and (3) recreational, accommodation, and educational facilities. The following sections describe subsequent efforts to attach population counts to each of these locations.

Residents

Burns and others (2011) used 2000 Census data, but residential population in this report is based on block group data from the 2010 U.S. Census (U.S. Census Bureau, 2012). According to the 2010 data, there are 5,711 households and 10,600 residents distributed across the study region. Because several of the hazard zones are significantly smaller than the U.S. Census block group data, the population data needed to be disaggregated. Two approaches to disaggregating the population data are described here.

One common approach to disaggregating population data is an "intelligent" dasymetric mapping technique based on NLCD land-cover data (Mennis 2003; Sleeter and Gould, 2007). This approach disaggregates population values from census totals by applying an interpolated areal weight to four population-density classes (high, medium, low, and uninhabited) related to various land-cover classes. The assignment of land-cover classes to the four population-density classes is done by the user and significantly influences final results. For example, the study area is heavily forested (fig. 2) and areas classified as developed in the NLCD are primarily along the U.S. Highway 26 corridor, trailhead parking lots, and major roads in the various communities. If high-intensity developed cells in NLCD data are assumed to be the same as high-density development in the dasymetric modeling, and if forested areas are ruled out as population locations, then resident population would be assigned incorrectly to Highway 26 and parking lots (for example, Burns and others, 2011). To resolve this issue, one could use ancillary road data (either separate road files or road polygons in the parcel data) to exclude these areas from consideration in the dasymetric modeling.

A pie-chart summarizing the percentage of structures in the enhanced MSA data organized by the various NLCD classes (fig. 5) indicates that most residential structures are in areas presumed in previous dasymetric studies to have no population, such as forest, water, wetland, barren land, and developed open space (Mennis and Hultgren, 2006; Reibel and Agrawal, 2007). For example, 51 percent of residential structures are in areas classified as forest and 23 percent are in areas classified as open-space developed—land-cover classes often assigned to an uninhabited population density class during dasymetric mapping (Sleeter, 2004; Mennis and Hultgren, 2006). The presence of structures in certain classes, such as water and wetland, may be due to floating homes (for example, a permanent houseboat) but more likely indicate a resolution or locational accuracy issue with the NLCD.

Because home locations were georeferenced within the enhanced MSA dataset, residential locations did not need to be modeled. Dasymetric-mapping techniques using midresolution land cover (such as NLCD) were unnecessary and, if employed improperly (for example, Burns and others, 2011), likely would lead to population-exposure errors. Instead, block group population data were disaggregated across the landscape, in a hybrid binary approach, by using the points classified as residential addresses in the MSA data. Population was assigned *only* to address point locations, and an areal weight value was determined for each residence based on census records. This was done by dividing block group population values by the number of addresses within the block group. For example, if a block group had a population of 12 people and there were 4 addresses within the block group, then it was assumed that there were 3 people at each address. Although this method disaggregates population from large areal units to actual residences, it assumes equal populations at each residence, which is not likely because some homes may have children or extended families and others may not. Subsequent population-exposure estimates, therefore, should be considered only first approximations, and follow-up work to identify population counts at specific addresses may be warranted in areas of high hazards.

There were several areas where buildings contained multiple addresses; therefore, a map showing residential population data using the address points would be difficult to decipher because of stacked and overlapping points (for example, fig. 4). Although subsequent exposure estimates were made using the original point data, a 30-meter raster grid of residential population data was created to simplify the visualization of population distributions across the study area. The number of residents in each 30-meter grid cell is the population sum for all of the address points in that cell (fig. 6). As compared to results from the first disaggregation method described, results from the address-point-based areal weighting technique reflect higher residential population counts among grid cells coinciding with multiple residential address locations. Data-quality checks, based on follow-up high-resolution imagery interpretation and fieldwork, showed the population modeling of this second method to be a reasonable estimation.

Two focus maps of residential population at 30-meter pixel resolution are provided for Welches (fig. 7A) and Government Camp (fig. 7B). These maps illustrate the methodology's ability to identify high-density areas that reflect apartment complexes, townhome developments, and condominium units. Figure 7 also demonstrates the methodology's ability to properly assign population to neighborhoods as opposed to the Highway 26 corridor, as can happen if dasymetric mapping techniques are used incorrectly (for example, see Burns and others, 2011).

To allow comparison of population numbers across the entire study area, a raster with 300-meter pixel resolution of residential population was generated (fig. 8A). Clustering of residents is observed along valley lows in the VMH and at the base of the mountain in Government Camp. Residents in the less rugged western portion of the study area (outside the City of Sandy) are much more dispersed.

Employees

The number, type, and distribution of employees within the study area were identified using the 2009 InfoGroup Employer Database, which is a proprietary business database that includes employee counts, location (address and latitude/longitude coordinates), generated sales volume, and business type based on the North American Industrial Classification System (NAICS; appendix A). Linking this data to the MSA records first involved joining data based on street addresses. Manual editing was based on imagery interpretation, Internet queries, and fieldwork for businesses with incomplete information or multiple records. For businesses with multiple records in the database, it was determined if records were duplications (and if so, duplicates were removed), or if distinct businesses existed but shared an address or existed within a larger company (for example, restaurants, gift shops, accommodations, and rental shops within a ski resort).

Manual examination and editing of the business data for this area yielded 323 georeferenced businesses that employ 3,149 people. Of the original data, some businesses could not be used in the exposure analysis owing to lack of address (11 percent), or because they had a U.S. Post Office box as a mailing address (4 percent). In addition to estimating employee exposure to various hazards, the types of employees in these zones are noted based on NAICS sectors, an indicator commonly used by the U.S. Bureau of Labor Statistics (2012) to assess economic trends. Similar to the residential data, business data attached to point locations were used in subsequent exposure estimates. A 300-meter-resolution map of employee population (fig. 8B) indicates that much of the region's workforce is focused in Welches and Government Camp and at certain businesses, such as Timberline Lodge, on the southern flank of Mount Hood.

Service Populations

As discussed earlier, several types of visitors temporarily come into the study area to enjoy various services or recreational opportunities. Analysis of this service population focused on the following groups.

- *Overnight visitors* are presumed to be primarily tourists and estimates of their numbers are based on occupancy at hotels, motels, resorts, bed and breakfast businesses, and vacation-home rentals,
- *Daytime visitors to recreation sites* are likely to be a mix of residents and tourists, and estimates of their numbers are based on attendance at public parks, private camps, U.S. Forest Service campgrounds and trailheads, and several tourist attractions, such as Mount Hood Skibowl, Timberline Lodge and Ski Area, Summit Ski Area, and the Mount Hood Cultural Center and Museum,
- *Dependents* are presumed to be residents, and estimates of their numbers are based on attendance at several schools (Welches Elementary, Firwood Elementary, Welches Middle School, and the Mount Hood Academy) and other facilities (Mount Hood Senior Center, the Mt. Hood Co-op Preschool, and Hoodland Children's Center).

Estimates of venue attendance were gathered through field work, email contact, and phone interviews. Business owners, property managers, school district managers, and center directors (for example, community centers) were asked to provide average monthly attendance totals, as well as peak daily estimates if available. U.S. Forest Service permit data (U.S. Forest Service, unpub. data, 2012) provided insight on attendance at some campgrounds and trailheads. Visitor estimates provided by businesses in the study area include daily estimates (Whispering Woods Resort, The Resort at the Mountain, and the Mount Hood Cultural Center and Museum), seasonal estimates (Mount Hood Skibowl) and annual estimates (Timberline Lodge and Ski Area). Several businesses did not provide any visitor estimates because they could not be reached (for example, private vacation rental homes), lacked visitor records, or lacked interest in study participation. Estimates, therefore, should be considered first approximations and not definitive statements of service populations.

Service-population magnitudes were estimated seasonally based upon local knowledge of the peak tourist periods: winter (December through February), spring (March through May), summer (June through August), and fall (September through November). Collected attendance data was arranged by season and calculated into the common unit of a monthly average because that was the most common unit used by businesses. For example, among each participating venue, the seasonal monthly average for summer was calculated by: (1) determining the attendance totals in June, July, and August; (2) adding the individual monthly totals together; and (3) dividing the seasonal grand total by three to obtain an average. Overnight visitors to the study area range from a low of 11,000 people per fall month to a peak of 34,000 people per summer month. Daytime visitors to recreation sites average from approximately 27,000 people per fall month to 129,300 people per winter month. Resident dependents at educational facilities total 549 people per fall, winter, and spring months and 93 people per summer month. These values are general trends in seasonal populations and actual attendance numbers for a given month may be higher than the calculated seasonal average. For example:

- Summertime average monthly attendance at The Resort at the Mountain is approximately 4,500, but can exceed 6,100 visitors in July;
- Summertime average monthly attendance at the U.S. Forest Service Trillium Lake Campground is approximately 5,400, but can reach 8,400 in August; and
- Wintertime average monthly attendance at the Summit Ski Area is approximately 3,900 yet January attendance can exceed 4,300.

Peak monthly attendance values from exposure analyses were omitted because not all venues were able to provide consistent visitor data, and for those that could, an individual venue's peak month could differ. Calculated monthly averages reported for seasonal populations are, in general, conservative estimates of the overall service population within the study area and are meant to provide insight on seasonal trends.

The monthly average-attendance values presented in this study can be translated into estimates of daily population, by consideration of the relevant population group. A daily estimate for overnight visitors and daytime visitors at recreation sites, can be calculated by dividing the seasonal monthly average value by thirty days (chosen as the length for an average month). Although they are easy to calculate, daily estimates for high-volume tourist destinations will have varying levels of accuracy because they underestimate populations on peak tourist days (weekends and holidays) and overestimate them on other days (weekdays and days with inclement weather). The dependent population monthly averages are based largely upon the number of children within the local public schools—values that reflect a general constant weekday attendance of school age children. Thus, daily estimates of dependent population attendance at local educational facilities are roughly equivalent to the seasonal monthly averages and do not require further calculations.

As was the case with the residential and employee data, service-population information was attached to point locations in the enhanced MSA data and exposure analyses were performed. Reporting a total number of tourist attractions is complex because of variations in how multistructures were mapped for the MSA dataset, such as multiple rental units within a resort being identified separately at one resort and collectively at another resort. The study area includes 1,068 recreational-site units which can be effectively summarized by 574 host facilities, of which 521 are lodging sites and 53 are recreation sites. Many of the public venues occur between the VMH area and Government Camp, including clusters of private vacation homes along the Zigzag River.

Service populations also vary during the day. To demonstrate this variability, raster grids were created to visualize attendance numbers for daytime visitors to recreation sites, schoolchildren and community-center attendees (fig. 9A), and overnight visitors (fig. 9B). There is variability at all times throughout the year; however, for illustrative purposes, only the variation during summer months is shown in this report. Overall, the maps suggest how variable the distribution of people enjoying the landscape can be between daytime and nighttime. Daytime visitors are more widely dispersed than nighttime visitors, which are fairly concentrated in Welches and Government Camp.

Road Volume

Vehicle-count data from recorders along Highway 26 (Oregon Department of Transportation, 2012) were analyzed to help understand population fluctuations in and out of the study area. This study focused on hourly data recorded from 2009 at Station 03_006 of the Oregon Department of Transportation (ODOT) Transportation Monitoring Program because it is on Highway 26 between the communities of Zigzag and Government Camp (fig. 1) and, therefore, is a good indicator of traffic conditions into the study area. Data recorded hourly was aggregated to daily totals, including the maximum number of vehicles within one hour on a given day (fig. 10A) and the total number of vehicles on that same day(fig. 10B). Vehicle counts, generally ranging between 2,000 and 12,000, are provided for eastbound traffic heading toward Government Camp (shown in black) and westbound traffic heading toward Sandy and Portland (shown in red). For example, 1,391 vehicles were counted in one hour traveling eastbound on the morning of Saturday, April 4 (fig. 10A), suggesting the peak traffic likely was due to snow-sport recreationists heading up to the mountains. The highest number of vehicles heading westbound (towards Portland) recorded in one hour was 1,307 vehicles and occurred on April 5, the day after the eastbound maximum value, suggesting that it represents people heading home to the Portland area. The one-day offset suggests many of these people spent the night in the study area, but also may include people driving westbound from destinations east of the study area such as Bend, Oreg.

The highest total number of vehicles recorded in one day was 11,368 vehicles traveling westbound on Monday, May 25, which was Memorial Day, suggesting a peak from holiday traffic returning to the Portland area (fig. 10B). The highest daily number of total vehicles traveling eastbound (9,914 vehicles) occurred on the previous Friday, May 22, the start of the holiday weekend. In both daily maximum per hour and daily totals, higher numbers were recorded for eastbound traffic than for westbound traffic. This may be due to multiple days of eastbound traffic into the area preceding a weekend (for example, Thursday through Sunday), many people possibly staying overnight in the area, and vehicles collectively leaving on Sunday westbound back to the Portland area.

The influence of holidays and weekends also is apparent when daily westbound vehicle counts are subtracted from eastbound counts for both daily maximum counts per hour (fig. 10C) and daily total counts (fig. 10D). For illustrative purposes, positive values indicate eastbound traffic was greater than westbound traffic at a given time and negative values indicate westbound traffic was greater. In both figures 10C and 10D, the peaks throughout the year typically are associated with Fridays, when people are traveling eastbound to recreation sites, and troughs are typically associated with Sundays, when people are returning to the Portland area. One exception is traffic associated with Memorial Day, which occurred on a Monday and resulted in maximum westbound traffic on this day. The highest traffic numbers are related to weekends for Memorial Day, the Fourth of July, Labor Day, and Thanksgiving.

Population Exposure to Natural Hazards

In addition to dynamic populations, the study area also is home to dynamic natural processes that have shaped the landscape, including volcanic and landslide activity at Mount Hood, repeated flooding and migration of the Sandy River floodplain, and wildfires in the surrounding forests. During the past decades, residents have contended with flooding, wildfires, and concern regarding volcanic unrest, especially in the wake of Mount St. Helens' 1980 eruption (Clackamas County, Oregon, 2002, p. 1-1). With the growing development and tourism in the study area, these natural processes pose increasing threats to people and property.

GIS-based analysis of population data (for example, homes, businesses, tourist attractions, and educational facilities) focused on determining if these locations (depicted as points) were inside hazard zones (depicted as polygons). Hazards of interest include flooding, wildfires, and volcanism owing to data availability and county interest. The following sub-sections describe each of these hazards, the hazard zones used in the population-exposure analysis, and the results of this analysis[2].

Population-exposure estimates in this report are meant to provide insight on general trends in the area and to support emergency-management planning. They are not definitive statements of population dynamics or mortality estimates for several reasons. First, exposure estimates assume that people are located where they are expected to be during an actual event—for example, residents are at their homes and not at work, the local market, or on a hiking trail. In addition, emergency managers and at-risk

---

[2]A direct comparison of population-exposure estimates to those presented in Burns and others (2011) was not done because of previously-discussed issues of data alignment and accuracy, their use and assumptions in dasymetric mapping, varying time periods for U.S. Census data, their exclusion of service populations, differences in study areas, and varying hazard zones (to be discussed in subsequent sections). Population-exposure estimates for each hazard in Burns and others (2011) are summarized for their entire three-county study area; therefore, comparisons to just the upper Sandy River study area are not possible.

populations likely will have some level of advance notice and warning of floods, wildfires, and volcanic eruptions (for example, rising flood stages before a flood, a fire ignition in an uninhabited part of the region, or increasing seismic activity before an eruption); therefore, there likely will be opportunities to move people and some property out of harm's way. Second, not all recreation-related businesses provided attendance numbers; therefore, the magnitude of the service population is likely to be higher than reported here. Third, in disaggregating census population counts to individual addresses, residents were distributed evenly among the addresses within a census block group, but in reality this distribution is uneven. Additionally, employee-exposure estimates are based on the assumption that all employees are present at the same time, as opposed to working in shifts; therefore, actual employee exposure may be lower than reported results. Finally, the best available data was used, but the age of the data varied— 2001 NLCD, 2005 high-resolution photography of study region, 2005 wildfire-risk zones, 2008 flood- and volcano-hazard zones, 2009 employment data, and 2010 U.S. Census Block Group data. Given these issues with the input data, exposure estimates should be viewed as first approximations and as vehicles for follow-up work and deeper discussions within the emergency-management community.

Flood Hazards

Hazard Delineation

Clackamas County has a long recorded history of floods dating back to 1861, with most flooding occurring from October to April due to seasonal storms coming from the Pacific Ocean (Clackamas County, Oregon, 2002, p. 6-2). Floods are a significant hazard in the study area, especially along the Sandy River, which also experiences channel migration (Clackamas County, Oregon, 2007, p. 27). The most recent flooding event on January 16, 2011, damaged several homes, caused temporary closure of Lolo Pass Road, compromised the structural integrity of the new Zigzag River bridge, and resulted in significant changes to the Sandy River channel because of extensive bank erosion (KATU News, 2011; U.S. Geological Survey National Water Information System, 2012). A channel-migration hazard zone for the Sandy River was created (English and others, 2011), but was not included in this analysis owing to the concurrent timing of the work.

Flood-hazard zones for this study are based on the 2008 Federal Emergency Management Agency (FEMA) Digital Flood Insurance Rate Map (DFIRM) (Federal Emergency Management Agency, 2008), which is the basis of floodplain management, mitigation, and insurance determination for the National Flood Insurance Program (NFIP)[3]. DFIRM flood zones include 100-year and 500-year events, which reflect flood levels with 1 percent and 0.2 percent annual chance, respectively, of being equaled or exceeded in any single year (Federal Emergency Management Agency, 2012). Although 100-year flood data further delineate zones based on known and unknown base elevations, this study aggregated the two zones and focused on 100-year and 500-year zones (fig. 11). The 500-year flood zone depicted in figure 11 represents the extended area of flooding expected from a larger, lower probability event; therefore, potential flooding from this event would include the yellow and red areas. Flood-hazard zones are present along the Sandy River, Cedar Creek, Salmon River, Zigzag River, and Still Creek and are threats primarily in the fall, winter, and spring seasons. Population-exposure analysis focused on the number of people and community features in the two hazard zones. The only exception was for visitor populations at recreational areas, where a 0.25-mile GIS buffer was added on to the hazard zone. This was done because many recreational areas cover large areas but are mapped only as

---

[3]This varies from the flood-hazard zones used in Burns and others (2011), in which researchers developed their own 25- and 500-year flood hazard zones.

point locations (for example, trailheads recorded by the U.S. Forest Service). This buffer could be used to help identify recreational areas that may be impacted by future floods.

Population Exposure

There are between 381 and 537 households and 717 and 960 residents threatened by flood hazards depending upon the severity of the flood (100- versus 500-year events, respectively). This translates to approximately 7 percent of households and residents in the study area in the 100-year flood zone and as much as 10 percent of households and residents in the 500-year flood hazard zone (fig. 12). Business and employee exposure is much less—7 businesses and 6 employees are in the 100-year zone (2 percent and less than 1 percent, respectively) and up to 15 businesses and 36 employees are in the 500-year hazard zone (4 percent and 1 percent, respectively). Of the 36 employees in the flood-hazard zones, most are in business sectors related to utilities, manufacturing, and transportation and warehousing (fig. 13). Approximately 20 percent of all utility and manufacturing jobs in the study area are in the 500-year flood zone. No schools or community centers are within the flood-hazard zones.

There are 60 vacation homes and vacation-rental properties within the flood-hazard zones, and 77 percent of them (46 of 60) are in the 100-year flood hazard zone. Most of the vacation homes in the flood-hazard zones are concentrated along the Zigzag River and Still Creek near the town of Rhododendron. Lack of records on private vacation-home occupancy precludes the ability to estimate overnight attendance. Although no campgrounds, trailheads, or other recreational areas fall completely within the flood-hazard zones, the U.S. Forest Service Pioneer-Tollgate Campground and trailhead is within a quarter mile of the Zigzag River, and visitors in the area could be affected by a flood event along the river. Regarding the seasons most prone to flooding, this campground typically averages 173 visitors per month during fall, 62 visitors per month during spring, and is closed during winter. Flooding also could affect access to parts of trails, such as Castle Canyon, Zigzag Mountain #775, Flag Mountain, and Old Salmon River, although inclement weather conditions are likely to preclude much usage of these trails during flood generation.

Wildfire Hazards

Hazard Delineation

The majority of the study area is covered by the Mount Hood National Forest; therefore, wildfire is a prevalent risk. Greatest risks of wildfires are during late summer and early fall owing to high temperatures and low humidity (Clackamas County, Oregon, 2002, p. 8-5). Conditions favoring future wildfire disasters include fuel build up and increases in development at the wildland/urban interface (Clackamas County, Oregon, 2005, p. 2). The most recent wildfire occurring near the study area (on the northern flank of Mount Hood) was the Dollar Lake Fire which ignited by lightning on August 26, 2011. It led to a declaration of emergency and burned more than 6,300 acres of wilderness (KGW News, 2011; InciWeb Incident Information System, 2012).

Wildfire-hazard zones come from the 2005 Clackamas County Community Wildfire Protection Plan (Clackamas County, Oregon, 2005) and are actually wildfire relative-risk zones, based on available fuel loads, slope, aspect, elevation, weather, historic-fire occurrence, home density and community infrastructure, and protection capability (fire-response time and level of community preparedness). Risk zones used in this analysis include five relative categories (high, moderate-to-high, moderate, low-to-moderate, and low) (fig. 14). Although risk zones identify specific wildfire-risk characteristics at a specific location, fires ignited at one spot can spread quickly to other areas considered to have lower risk. Accordingly, the overall size of any future fire cannot be predicted. Fire-prevention efforts by

13

communities and the Hoodland Fire District also can reduce wildfire risk in specific locations; therefore, the wildfire-risk zones and subsequent population-exposure estimates should be viewed as first approximations and not as guarantees of either being directly impacted or spared impact from a future wildfire.

Wildfire-risk zones have been established across the entire study region and represent a perception of risk rather than a predicted area of impact. The greatest percentage of the study area is characterized as moderate-to-high wildfire risk (44 percent) followed by high wildfire risk (25 percent) (fig. 15A). Areas of lower risk are concentrated around river channels and in the western-most section of the study area (fig. 14). Overall, 90 percent of the study area is considered to have at least a moderate risk of wildfire.

Population Exposure

Although most of the study area is classified as moderate-to-high and high wildfire risk, the majority of homes and businesses (87 and 85 percent, respectively) are in areas classified as moderate wildfire risk or lower (fig. 15). The highest percentage of homes is in moderate wildfire-risk zones (53 percent) (fig. 15B). Of the 323 businesses in the study area, the greatest percentage of them (33 percent) is in low wildfire-risk zones (fig. 15C). Although only 15 percent of businesses are in moderate-to-high or high wildfire-risk zones, these businesses account for 51 percent of the study-area workforce (fig. 15D).

The various business sectors are not exposed equally to wildfire risk. The distribution of employees, by business sector, in the various wildfire-risk zones indicates that some sectors (for example, education services, finance and insurance, and retail trade) have high percentages of their workforce in moderate-to-high and high wildfire-risk zones (fig. 16). More than 50 percent of the workforce within the following business sectors is exposed to moderate or higher risk for wildfire: construction, retail trade, professional/scientific services, education services, and health care/social assistance. Wildfire risk also is high among employees in the education-services sector, which includes businesses outside of the public school system, with nearly 90 percent of the workforce exposed to moderate-to-high wildfire risk or greater.

Evaluation of the wildfire risk posed to service populations focused only on those seasons coincident with wildfire occurrence (summer and fall). Figure 17 shows charts of exposure to wildfire risk among the three service-population categories—dependents, overnight visitors, and daytime visitors to recreation sites. Owing to local public schools being in session, the average monthly attendance among school children and individuals at community centers is much higher in the fall and reaches a combined attendance estimate of 1,000 people (fig. 17A). Schools are in varying levels of wildfire risk including low (Mount Hood Academy and Welches Elementary), low-to-moderate (Welches Middle School and Firwood Elementary School) and moderate (community center). In general, the majority of the dependent seasonal population has either a low-to-moderate or low risk of wildfire. In the fall, for example, approximately two-thirds of the dependent population has a low-to-moderate level of wildfire risk.

Overnight visitors (fig. 17B) and daytime visitors to recreation sites (fig. 17C) are much more prevalent in the study area during the summer months and account for tens of thousands of people. There are, on average, approximately 34,000 overnight visitors at lodging facilities during a summer month and 11,000 overnight visitors during a month in the fall (approximatly 1,133 and 367 overnight visitors per day, respectively). Although wildfire danger exposes many more people in the summer months, 71 percent of these visitors are exposed to either a low-to-moderate or low level of wildfire risk. Thirty percent of the lodging facilities are within moderate or higher wildfire-risk areas

The only accommodations in high wildfire risk are private vacation homes which do not have attendance records. Moderate-to-high wildfire risk exists for Timberline Lodge and some units at both The Resort at the Mountain and Whispering Woods Resort. Overall, the majority of the overnight visitor seasonal population has either a low-to-moderate or low level of wildfire risk, but those with greater exposure (moderate and higher) equate to an average of about 10,000 and 4,000 people per month in the summer and fall, respectively

Among the daytime visitors to recreation sites, the summertime monthly average is roughly 99,000 people and exceeds the average monthly attendance estimate of 27,000 for the fall (about 3,300 and 900 daytime visitors to recreation sites per day, respectively). The percentage of daytime visitors to recreation sites exposed to wildfire risk of moderate level or higher is roughly the same for both summer and fall (58 and 59 percent, respectively); however, on average, 58,000 people per month are vulnerable to this wildfire risk in the summer and only 16,000 people per month are at similar risk in the fall (approximating 1,933 and 533 daytime visitors to recreation sites per day, respectively). Wildfire risk for seasonal attendance of daytime visitors to recreation sites was evaluated at sites such as public parks, private camps, U.S. Forest Service campgrounds and trailheads, and tourist attractions like Mount Hood Ski Bowl, Timberline Lodge and Ski Area, and the Mount Hood Cultural Center and Museum. Those sites with higher risk of wildfire include some U.S. Forest Service campgrounds (Trillium Lake and Lost Creek) and trailheads (Dry Fir/Veda Lake, Eureka Peak, Grave Trail, West ZZ-Burnt/Cast Lake, Upper Horseshoe, and North Burnt Lake) and portions of Windells Snowboard Camp and the Mount Hood Summer Ski Camp (specifically at the Lodges at Salmon River).

Volcanic Hazards

Hazard Delineation

Mount Hood is located on the northeastern edge of Clackamas County and is a composite volcano that consists of lava flows, lava domes, and related volcaniclastic debris (Scott and others, 1997a). Three eruptive periods have been identified for Mount Hood in the past 15,000 years, including the Polallie (12,000–15,000 years ago) the Timberline (1,400–1,800 years ago), and the Old Maid (A.D. 1781 and lasting about a decade) (Scott and others, 1997a, b; Pierson and others, 2011). Although no major eruptive events have occurred at Mount Hood since the late 18th century, there have been reports of steam emissions and minor tephra falls in the mid-19th century, and small lahars (volcanic debris flows), small debris avalanches, and short-lived swarms of small earthquakes in recent decades (Scott and others, 1997a; Gardner and others, 2000). The likelihood of a Mount Hood eruption originating near Crater Rock, the youngest lava dome on the mountain, is estimated to be between 1 in 15 and 1 in 30 in the next 30 years. The likelihood of an extreme event is even lower—1 in 10,000 in the next 30 years, but such an event would be catastrophic for the region (Scott and others, 1997b).

Volcano hazard zones are derived from Scott and others (1997b) with digital updating by Schilling and others (2008) and include proximal and distal hazards with subclassification based upon vent location, magnitude of event, and probability of inundation[4]. In this study detailed hazard designations are reclassified into three categories—proximal hazards, distal hazards for a typical scenario, and distal hazards for a worst-case scenario (maximum credible lahar) (fig. 18). These hazard zones, by design, are not necessarily indicative of impact from one specific event and simply represent probable areas under threat. In addition, although population estimates are provided for "no volcano hazard" areas, these areas should not be considered completely hazard-free as too many uncertainties

---

[4]This varies from the volcanic-hazard zones used in Burns and others (2011), in which researchers developed their own lahar-hazard zones.

exist in the source, magnitude, and mobility of future events (Scott and others, 1997b). Again, population estimates within hazard zones are for emergency-planning purposes as volcanic eruptions often are preceded by indicators of unrest which allow emergency managers time to initiate emergency-response efforts.

Proximal hazards can travel from source to the hazard boundary in less than 30 minutes and include lava flows, ballistic fragments, pyroclastic flows (hot, dense flows of rock debris and gas generated by collapses of growing lava domes), debris avalanches (rapid landslides from the steep upper slopes of the volcano), and near-source volcanic lahars (volcanic mud flows). Given the topographic relief of Mount Hood, a large pyroclastic flow—generated by the collapse of a substantial lava dome at the Crater Rock site—could theoretically inundate Timberline Lodge and Government Camp, Oreg., in less than 30 minutes time (Brantley and Scott, 1993; William Scott, oral communication, June 2012) (fig. 19). Landslides of volcanic debris (volcanic debris surges) are a perceived hazard on the steep slopes of the study area's mountainous terrain (Clackamas County, Oregon, 2002) and can be triggered by events other than volcanic eruptions. For example, within the White River valley of Mount Hood, volcanic debris surges related to glacial melt water have forced closures of the Oregon Route 35 bridge 20 times since 1907 (Anderson and others, 2006). The most recent White River valley landslide event was generated in November 2006 by a major rainstorm. It caused major damage to the bridge, cut a new channel through the highway, and moved 2 million cubic yards of mud, debris, and boulders larger than pickup trucks (Hood River News, 2012).

Distal volcanic hazards refer to lahars that can travel tens of miles down valleys from the volcano. Two levels of distal lahar hazards exist (referred to as typical and worst-case scenarios) based on frequency and magnitude. As was the case with the 100- and 500-year flood data, the worst-case distal lahar-hazard zone includes the inundation areas associated with a typical event. Distal lahar-hazard zones are not tied to a specific single event, and eruptive periods that last for months to years can include events of a wide range of sizes. In addition, sedimentation from numerous lahars associated with an eruptive period can fill valleys over time and cause wider inundation of volcanic material (William Scott, oral communication, June 2012). Distal hazards can range from a chronic problem that gradually encroaches on broad areas to single catastrophic events of large size that inundate all or most of a hazard zone. Monitoring likely will detect the onset of unrest prior to a large event, providing opportunities to protect people and some property.

Population Exposure

Proximal volcanic hazards threaten 1,315 homes and 104 businesses, representing 1,501 residents and 2,041 employees (fig. 20). The percentages of all homes and businesses for the study area that are in the proximal hazard zones are similar (23 and 32 percent, respectively); however, the percentages for residents and employees in these homes and businesses diverge substantially. Although 23 percent of study-area homes are in the proximal hazard zone, only 14 percent of residents are in that area, suggesting that these homes do not contain many families (fig. 20A). Conversely, the 32 percent of study-area businesses that are in the proximal hazard zone represent 65 percent of the study-area workforce, suggesting these businesses on the flanks of the volcano are primary drivers for the local economy (fig. 20B and C).

Distal volcanic hazards also pose significant threats to downstream communities and businesses (fig. 20). The typical distal hazard zone contains 2,047 homes and 99 businesses, representing 3,834 residents and 617 employees. This accounts for 36 percent of all households and residents in the area, 31 percent of businesses, and 20 percent of employees. The decrease in employee exposure relative to the proximal hazard suggests the larger businesses are on the upper reaches of Mount Hood (for example, Timberline Lodge) and smaller businesses (such as restaurants and retail stores) are more characteristic in the foothill valleys. A worst-case distal hazard zone would increase the number of threatened homes and businesses, but the difference in those exposed does not exceed 10 percent among the different categories. The worst-case scenario includes an additional 503 homes (9 percent of study area), 1,055 residents (10 percent), 34 businesses (10 percent), and 91 employees (2 percent) to those already accounted for in the typical distal hazard zone. Assuming, the potential for typical or worst-case scenarios, volcanic hazards threaten 3,362–3,865 homes (59–68 percent) and 203–237 businesses (63–73 percent). These homes and businesses represent 5,335–6,390 residents (50–60 percent) and 2,658–2,749 employees (84–87 percent). Again, the distinction in population-exposure estimates between a typical and worst-case scenario is not dramatically different because most development occurs in the low-lying areas along the river valleys and therefore could be impacted by any distal event, regardless of magnitude or event duration.

Business exposure to volcano hazards varies by sector (fig. 21). Many business sectors have a high percentage of their employees in the proximal hazard zone, such as education services (95 percent), arts, entertainment, and recreation (95 percent), public administration (89 percent), and accommodation and food services (65 percent). These businesses are threatened by volcanic hazards regardless of the magnitude of related distal hazards. Other business sectors, such as information, finance and insurance, real estate, health care, and social assistance, are primarily in the typical distal hazard zones. A worst-case scenario event would not substantially change the exposure of most business sectors, except for agriculture (0–15 percent of study-area employees in this sector), transportation and warehousing (33–77 percent of employees), and construction (45–68 percent of employees).

Of the 579 locations with service populations in the study area, 460 of them (approximately 80 percent) are in proximal volcanic-hazard zones, including 420 lodging facilities, 36 recreation sites, and 4 schools or community centers (table 1). Distal hazard zones include a range of 15 lodging facilities and 5 recreation sites (typical scenario) to 96 lodging facilities and 8 recreation sites (worst-case scenario). This suggests that 8– 97 percent of non-residential addresses, depending on hazard scenario (typical and worst-case scenarios, respectively), are in areas prone to volcanic hazards.

Table 1. Volcano-hazard exposure by service population facilities, Mount Hood region of Clackamas County, Oregon.

Volcano hazards	Total service-population locations	Lodging	Day-use recreation	Schools and community centers
Proximal hazards	460	420	36	4
Distal lahar hazard (typical scenario)	20	15	5	0
Distal lahar hazards (worst-case scenario)	104	96	8	0
No hazard	15	5	9	1
Study area total	579	521	53	5

Unlike floods and wildfires, volcanic eruptions are not seasonal and could occur at any time of year; therefore, volcano exposure to service populations is presented for all four seasons (fig. 22). Populations at the schools and community centers are consistent throughout the school year (nearly 550 people) and decrease only in the summer months (fig. 22A). Summer months have the greatest number of overnight visitors, with approximately 22,000 people in the proximal zone, 10,750 people in the typical distal hazard zone, plus an additional 820 people if the distal scenario is a worst-case-scenario event (fig. 22B). This is approximately 34,000 people per summer month, or 1,100 people per day. Approximately two-thirds of overnight visitors are in the proximal hazard zone, including all lodging within Government Camp and much of that within the VMH area. As was the case with extreme flood events, the distinction in population exposure between typical and worst-case-scenario events is not substantial (an addition of approximately 2 percent of overnight visitors). Winter months have the second highest number of overnight visitors in volcanic-hazard zones (approximately 20,500 per month), followed by spring and fall months (12,500 and 11,000, respectively).

The number of daytime visitors to recreation sites in volcanic-hazard zones is greatest during winter months —approximately 129,300 people per month or 4,300 people per day (fig. 22C). The vast majority of these daytime visitors are in the proximal hazard zone (approximately 128,800 people per month), reflecting snow-sport activity on the upper flanks of Mount Hood. Summer months have the second highest number of daytime visitors to recreation sites in volcanic-hazard zones (approximately 94,000 people per month or 3,100 people per day on average), with about 82 percent in the proximal zone, 18 percent in the typical distal hazard zone, and a negligible additional percentage in the worst-case scenario event distal hazard zone. The number of daytime visitors to recreation sites in volcanic-hazard zones is less but still substantial during spring months (approximately 63,000 per month) and fall months (approximately 25,500 per month). Regardless of season, results suggest that the majority of seasonal populations are in the proximal hazard zone and that there is little difference in population exposure between typical and worst-case-scenarios for distal hazards. The proximal zone likely will be devoid of residents or visitors at the time of an event owing to the monitored period of volcanic unrest leading to an eruption.

Conclusions

This study, a collaboration of the U.S. Geological Survey and the Clackamas County Department of Emergency Management, evaluates community vulnerability to flood, wildfire, and volcano hazards within the VMH and Government Camp region of Clackamas County, Oreg. The work's intent is to develop methodology for exposure research, to improve understanding of community vulnerability, and to assist with further development of emergency plans and community-outreach activities. Documenting the composition and spatial distribution of populations within a rural, tourist-destination setting is challenging owing to the highly dynamic and dispersed nature of residents, employees, overnight visitors, daytime visitors to recreation sites, and dependents. Based on a geospatial analysis of population exposure to flood, wildfire, and volcanic hazards, the following conclusions can be made:

- The heavily forested landscape and limited development in study area would suggest low population; however, tens of thousands among the various population groups are present.

- Much of the development within the study region occurs in valley-floor areas, which increases the chance for residents, employees, and visitors to be exposed to flooding and distal (lahar) volcanic hazards.

- Visitors are a substantial component of the region's service population at any given time. Summer months are dominated by overnight visitors and winter months are dominated by daytime visitors to recreation sites.

- Flooding could impact up to 10 percent of homes and residents, 4 percent of businesses, and 1 percent of employees, depending on event magnitude. Population exposure to flood hazards within the study area does not increase dramatically with increasing flood severity—the difference in population exposed between a 100-year flood and a 500-year flood event scenario is 3 percent or less.

- Although the majority of the study area is classified as moderate-to-high or greater wildfire risk, most homes, businesses, and overnight accommodations are in areas classified as moderate wildfire risk or lower. Only 15 percent of businesses are within moderate-to-high or high wildfire-risk areas, but the employees on site account for 51 percent of the local workforce. These areas also attract approximately 60 percent of daytime visitors to recreation sites where they are exposed to moderate or higher wildfire risk.

- A period of eruption at Mount Hood could impact up to 68 percent of homes, 60 percent of residents, 73 percent of businesses, and 87 percent of employees. A worst-case scenario would increase population exposure during a typical event, but the increase is not substantial—typically 10 percent or less of an increase in population exposed. Service-population exposure to volcano hazards is largest in the proximal hazard zone, including 65 percent of the local workforce, 80 percent of educational facilities, 82–100 percent of daytime visitors to recreation sites (summer and winter month averages, respectively), and approximately two-thirds of overnight visitors.

- Factors adding complexity to emergency response and evacuation efforts include: (1) thousands of vehicles passing through the region on any given day, (2) several tourist draws located entirely in the proximal volcanic-hazard zone (such as Mount Hood Skibowl, Timberline Lodge and Ski Area, and Summit Ski Area), and (3) the dependence of the local road network on the single-corridor outlet of U.S. Highway 26.

This project explored research methods, information synthesis, and the various geographic-data inputs required to better estimate population distributions of residents, employees, and visitors within a rural community setting. By better understanding how much of the population within Clackamas County around Mount Hood is exposed to natural hazards, public officials can identify locations within communities and their respective business sectors that may require additional preparedness, mitigation, recovery planning, and outreach activities. The information provided in this report is intended to enhance the dialogue regarding societal risk and resilience in areas prone to multiple natural hazards.

Acknowledgments

We specifically acknowledge Jay Wilson (Clackamas County Emergency Management Department) for his collaboration since the project's inception; his thoughtful contributions toward this report are greatly appreciated. Research work was supported by the U.S. Geological Survey Geographic Analysis and Monitoring Program. William Scott (U.S. Geological Survey Cascade Volcano Observatory), Kelly Neumeier (Clackamas County Technology Services, Geographic Information Systems Division), and Cindy Kolomechuk (Oregon Department of Forestry) gave insightful reviews of this manuscript. We also thank Dave Ramsey (U.S. Geological Survey Cascade Volcano Observatory) for insights on appropriate recoding of volcano hazards GIS data.

References Cited

Anderson, D.A., DeRoo, T.G., and Hedeen, C.D., 2006, Response to 1998 debris flow in the upper White River valley, Oregon, Oregon Geology, v. 67, no. 1, Fall 2006, p. 7–10, accessed May 30, 2012, at http://www.oregongeology.org/pubs/og/OGv67n01.pdf .

Anderson, J.R., Hardy, E.E., Roach, J.T., and Witmer, R.E., 1976, A land use and land cover classification system for use with remote sensor data: U.S. Geological Survey Professional Paper 964, accessed May 30, 2012, at http://landcover.usgs.gov/pdf/anderson.pdf .

Australian Bureau of Statistics, 2008, Information paper—Population Concepts, 2008: Australia, no. 3107.0.55.006, accessed July 24, 2012, at http://www.abs.gov.au/AUSSTATS/abs@.nsf/DetailsPage/3107.0.55.0062008?OpenDocument .

Brantley, S.R., and Scott, W.E., 1993, The danger of collapsing lava domes: Lessons for Mount Hood, Oregon: Earthquakes and Volcanoes, v. 24, no. 6, p. 244–269.

Bureau of Labor Statistics, 2012, Overview of BLS statistics on employment: U.S. Department of Labor, accessed May 4, 2012, at http://www.bls.gov/bls/employment.htm .

Burns, W.J., Hughes, K.L.B., Olson, K.V., McClaughry, J.D., Mickelson, K.A., Coe, D.E., English, J.T., Roberts, J.T., Lyles Smith, R.R., and Madin, I.P., 2011,Multi-hazard and risk study for the Mount Hood region, Multnomah, Clackamas, and Hood River counties: Oregon, Oregon Department of Geology and Mineral Industries, Open-File Report O-11-16, accessed May 30, 2012, at http://www.oregongeology.org/pubs/ofr/p-O-11-16.htm .

Clackamas County, Oregon, 2002, Clackamas County—Natural hazard mitigation plan, 302 p., accessed August 22, 2011, at http://scholarsbank.uoregon.edu/jspui/handle/1794/2341 .

Clackamas County, Oregon, 2007, The Clackamas County natural hazard mitigation plan, accessed August 30, 2012, at http://www.clackamas.us/emergency/naturalhazard html .

Clackamas County, Oregon, 2005, Clackamas County Community Wildfire Protection Plan, 119 p.

Clackamas County, Oregon, 2012, About Clackamas County, accessed May 2012 at, http://www.co.clackamas.or.us/about.htm .

Cook, Tricia, 1996, When ERP aren't enough—A discussion of issues associated with service population estimation: ABS Demongraphy Working Paper 1996, v. 4, accessed July 2012 at, http://www.abs.gov.au/ausstats/abs@ nsf/mf/3112.0 .

Cruden, D.M., 1991, A simple definition of a landslide: Bulletin of the International Association of Engineering Geology, no. 43, p. 27–29.

English, J.T., Coe, D.E., Chappell, R.D., 2011, Channel migration hazards maps for the Sandy River, Multnomah and Clackamas counties, Oregon, Oregon Department of Geology and Mineral Industries

(DOGAMI), Open-File Report O-11-13, accessed July 24, 2012, at
http://www.oregongeology.org/pubs/ofr/p-O-11-13.htm .

Federal Emergency Management Agency, 2008, Map Service Center: U.S. Department of Homeland Security, available at
https://msc fema.gov/webapp/wcs/stores/servlet/FemaWelcomeView?storeId=10001&catalogId=10001&langId=-1.

Federal Emergency Management Agency, 2012, Flood zones: NFIP Policy Index: U.S. Department of Homeland Security, accessed June 2012 at,
http://www.fema.gov/plan/prevent/floodplain/nfipkeywords/flood_zones.shtm .

Gardner, C.A., Scott, W.E., Major, J.J., and Pierson, T.C., 2000, Mount Hood—History and hazards of Oregon's most recently active volcano: U.S. Geological Survey Fact Sheet 060-00, accessed August 2012 at http://pubs.usgs.gov/fs/2000/fs060-00/ .

Homer, Collin, Dewiltz, Jon, Fry, Joyce, Coan, Michael, Hossain, Nazmul, Larson, Charles, Herold, Nate, McKerrow, Alexa, VanDriel, J. N., and Wickham, James, 2007, Completion of the 2001 National Land Cover Database for the Conterminous United States: Photogrammetric Engineering and Remote Sensing, v. 73, no. 4, p. 337–341, available at http://www mrlc.gov/nlcd2001.php.

Hood River News, 2012, Highway 35 improvement projects complete six years after washout—Bridge rededicated: Eagle Newspapers, Inc., accessed March 2013 at
http://www.hoodrivernews.com/news/2012/nov/13/highway-35-improvement-projects-complete-six-years/.

InciWeb Incident Information System, 2012, Final Dollar Lake Fire daily update 10-1-2011, accessed August 30, 2012, at http://www.inciweb.org/incident/2563/ .

InfoGroup, 2009, Employer database, available at http://referenceusagov.com/Static/Home .

KATU News, 2011, Sandy River flood 2011, January 17, 2011: Fisher Interactive Network, accessed May 30, 2012, at http://www.katu.com/younews/113991494.html .

KGW News, 2011, Oregon governor declares emergency amid wildfires, September 8, 2011: King Broadcasting Company, accessed August 30, 2012, at http://www.kgw.com/news/Governor-Will-Tour-Dollar-Lake-Fire-129500953 html .

Loveland, T.R., and Shaw, D.M., 1996, Multi-resolution land characterization—Building collaborative partnerships, in Scott, J.M., Tear, T.H., and Davis, F.W., eds., GAP Analysis—A landscape approach to biodiversity planning: Bethesda, Md., American Society for Photogrammetry and Remote Sensing, p. 79–85.

Mennis, J., 2003, Generating surface models of population using dasymetric mapping: The Professional Geographer, v. 55, no. 1, p. 31–42.

Mennis, J. and Hultgren, T., 2006, Intelligent dasymetric mapping and its application to areal interpolation: Cartography and Geographic Information Science, v. 33, no. 3, p. 179–194.

National Agriculture Imagery Program, 2005, Clackamas County, OR, U.S. Department of Agriculture, Aerial Photography Field Office, accessed November 2009 at http://www.fsa.usda.gov/FSA/apfoapp?area=home&subject=prog&topic=nai .

Oregon Department of Transportation, 2012, Traffic Counting Program: ODOT Transportation Data Section, accessed June 2012 at http://www.oregon.gov/ODOT/TD/TDATA/pages/tsm/tvt.aspx .

Oregon Blue Book, 2012, County populations—1970-2009: Oregon Secretary of State, accessed May 2010 at http://bluebook.state.or.us/local/populations/pop06.htm .

Pierson, T.C., Pringle, P.T., and Cameron, K.A., 2011, Magnitude and timing of downstream channel aggradation and degradation in response to a dome-building eruption at Mount Hood, Oregon: Geological Society of America Bulletin. v. 123, no. 1–2, p. 3–20, accessed August 2012 http://bulletin.geoscienceworld.org/cgi/content/full/123/1-2/3?ijkey=4xxL7.WGKnpY.&keytype=ref&siteid=gsabull .

Reibel, Michael, and Agrawal, Aditya, 2007, Areal interpolation of population counts using pre-classified land cover data: Population Research and Policy Review, v. 26, p. 619–613.

Schilling, S.P., Doelger, Sarah., Scott, W.E., Pierson, T.C., Costa, J.E., Gardner, C.A., Vallance, J.W., and Major, J.J., 2008, Digital data for volcano hazards for the Mount Hood region, Oregon (data to accompany U.S. Geological Survery Open-File Report 97-89), U.S. Geological Survey Open-File Report 2007-1222, accessed August 2012 at http://vulcan.wr.usgs.gov/Volcanoes/Hood/Hazards/OFR2007-1222/framework.html.

Scott, W.E., Gardner, C.A., Sherrod, D.R., Tilling, R.I., Lanphere, M.A., and Conrey, R.M., 1997a, Geologic history of Mount Hood Volcano, Oregon—A field-trip guidebook, U.S. Geological Survey Open-File Report 97-263, 38 p., accessed August 26, 2011, at http://vulcan.wr.usgs.gov/Volcanoes/Hood/Publications/OFR97-263/framework.html .

Scott, W.E., Pierson, T.C., Schilling, S.P., Costa, J.E., Gardner, C.A., Vallance, J.W., and Major, J.J., 1997b, Volcano hazards in the Mount Hood region, Oregon: U.S. Geological Survey Open-File Report 97-89, 14 p., available at http://vulcan.wr.usgs.gov/Volcanoes/Hood/Hazards/OFR97-89/framework html.

Sleeter, R., 2004, Dasymetric mapping techniques for the San Francisco Bay region, California: Urban and Regional Information Systems Association, Annual Conference, Reno, Nev., November 7–10, 2004 [Proceedings], available at http://geography.wr.usgs.gov/science/dasymetric/data/URISA_Journal.pdf.

Sleeter, R., and Gould, M., 2007, Geographic information system software to remodel population data using dasymetric mapping methods: U.S. Geological Survey Techniques and Methods 11-C2, 15 p., available at http://pubs.usgs.gov/tm/tm11c2/ .

Taylor, Barbara, 1998, Salmon and steelhead runs and related events of the Sandy River Basin—A historical perspective: Oreg., Portland General Electric, accessed July 25, 2012, at http://www.portlandgeneral.com/community_environment/initiatives/protecting_fish/sandy_river/docs/sandy_river_history_full.pdf .

U.S. Census Bureau, 2012, State & County Quickfacts: U.S. Department of Commerce, accessed May 30, 2012, at http://quickfacts.census.gov/qfd/index.html .

U.S. Department of Agriculture National Agriculture Imagery Program, 2009, Archived NAIP data: U.S. Department of Agriculture, Farm Service Agency, National Agriculture Imagery Program, accessed November 2009, at http://www.fsa.usda.gov/FSA/apfoapp?area=home&subject=maps&topic=arc.

U.S. Geological Survey The National Map, 2009, The National Map viewer and download platform: U.S. Geological Survey, The National Map, accessed November 2009, at http://nationalmap.gov/viewer.html.

U.S. Geological Survey National Water Information System, 2012, Surface Water for Oregon—Peak Streamflow, USGS 14142500 Sandy River BLW Bull Run River, NR Bull Run, OR: U.S. Geological Survey Water Resources, accessed May 2012, at http://nwis.waterdata.usgs.gov/or/nwis/peak?site_no=14142500&agency_cd=USGS&format=html .

Wood, Nathan, 2011, Understanding risk and resilience to natural hazards: U.S. Geological Survey Fact Sheet 2011-3008, 2 p.

Wood, N.J., and Good, J.W., 2004, Vulnerability of a port and harbor community to earthquake and tsunami hazards—The use of GIS in community hazard planning: Coastal Management, v. 32, no. 3, p. 243–269.

Zandbergen, P.A., and Ignizio, D.A., 2010, Comparison of dasymetric mapping techniques for small-area population estimates; Cartography and Geographic Information Science, v. 37, no. 3, p. 199–214.

Figure 1. Location maps of study area within Clackamas County, Oregon. Map *A* shows the county's location and interstate highway transportation routes within Oregon (metropolitan area of Portland, Oreg., marked with a dashed yellow line). Map *B* shows the county's topography with shaded relief (generated from a 10-meter digital elevation model) and location of study area (outlined in black) (U.S. Census Bureau, 2012). Data for roads, government boundaries, and shaded relief sourced from The National Map (U.S. Geological Survey, 2009). Features of study area shown on Map *C* with 2005 high-resolution photography (U.S. Department of Agriculture National Agriculture Imagery Program, 2009)—villages of unincorporated area (labeled in white), Mount Hood (labeled in black), and major highways (U.S. Route 26 and Oregon Route 35).

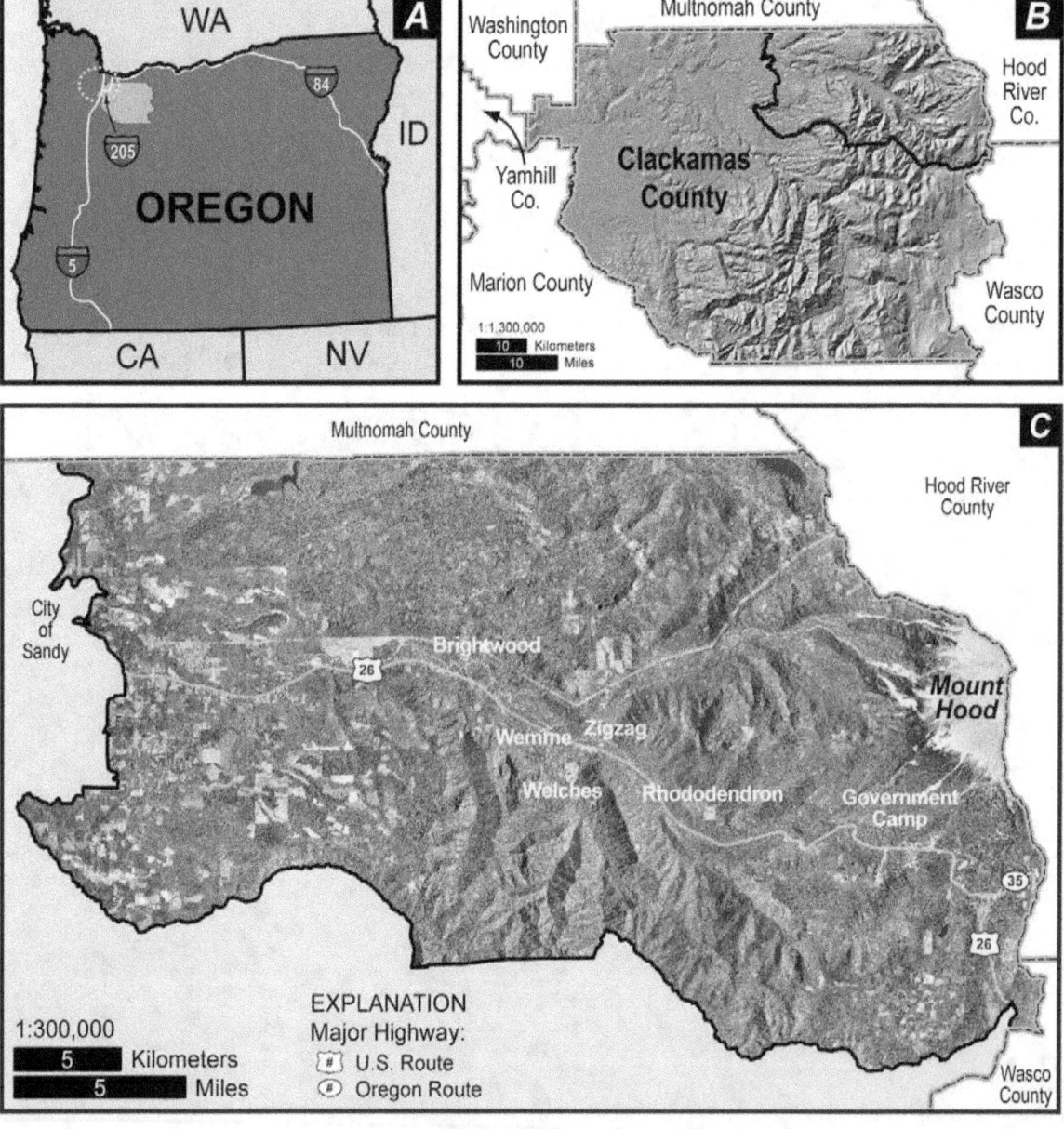

Figure 2. Map (*A*) and pie graph by area (*B*) of the land cover classification of the study area (National Land Cover Database, 2001), Clackamas County, Oregon.

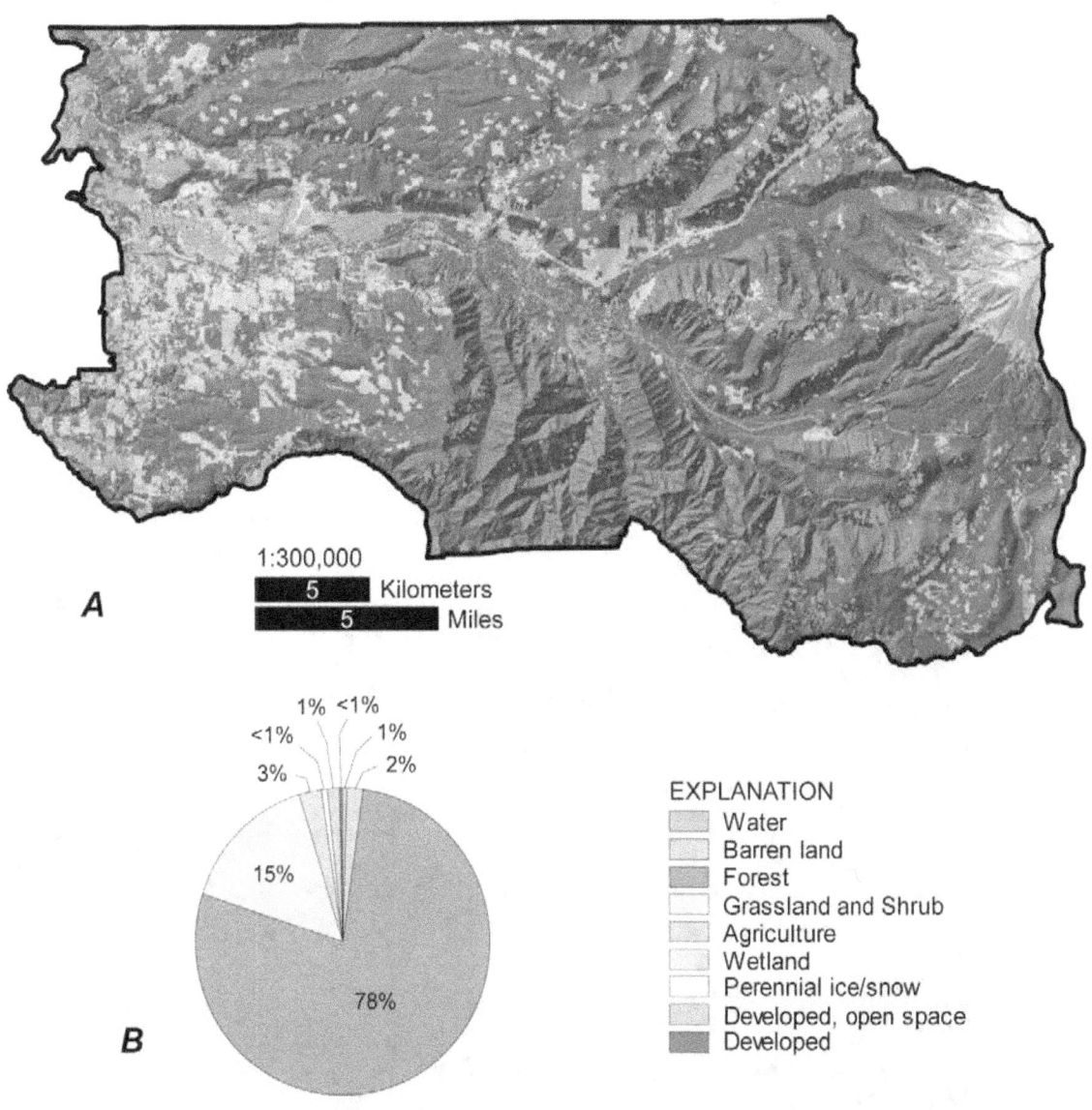

Figure 3. Images of the Villages at Mount Hood and Government Camp study area in Clackamas County, Oregon (U.S. Geological Survey photographs taken by A. Mathie): *A*, Government Camp, Oreg.; *B*, Hiking along U.S. Forest Service Mirror Lake Trail, located off U.S. Route 26 along western boundary of Government Camp, Oreg.; *C*, Golfing in Welches, Oreg.; *D*, "Hood to Coast" relay race start at Timberline Lodge, Government Camp, Oreg.; *E*, Mount Hood Skibowl winter resort and summer adventure park (Government Camp, Oreg.) with U.S. Highway 26 in foreground; *F*, U.S. Forest Service Trillium Lake Campground, located 4 miles south of Government Camp, Oreg. off U.S. Route 26; *G*, Festival information at Wildwood Recreation Site, located near Wemme, Oreg. on U.S. Route 26.

Figure 4. Map of categorized structure point data derived from Master Street Address (MSA) structure file, Clackamas County, Oregon.

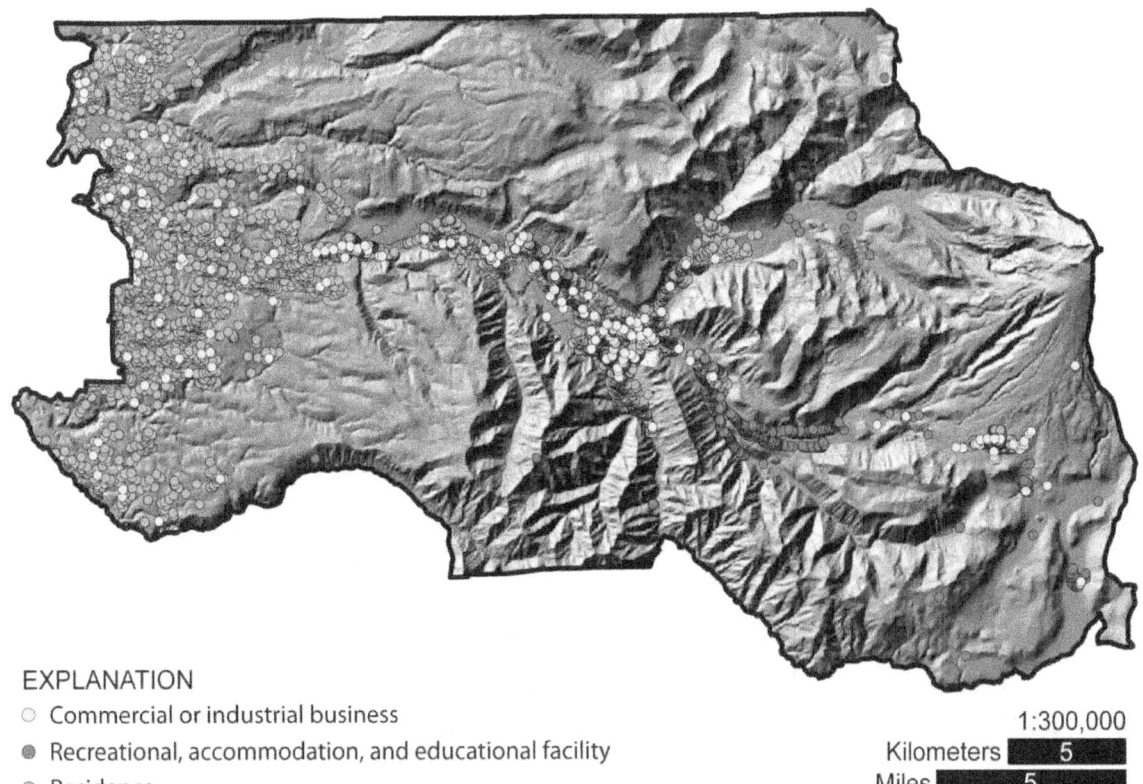

EXPLANATION
○ Commercial or industrial business
● Recreational, accommodation, and educational facility
◉ Residence

1:300,000
Kilometers ▮ 5
Miles ▮ 5

Figure 5. Distribution of residential structures by land cover class (based upon 2001 NLCD land cover), Clackamas County, Oregon. The total number of residences ("n-value") in the research area is 5,711, and residence counts associated with listed percentages are in parentheses.

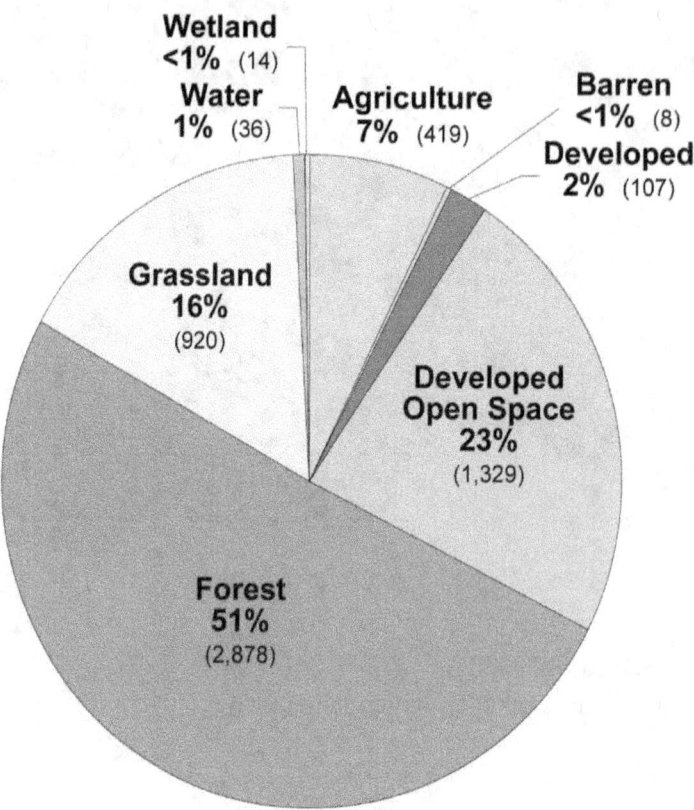

Figure 6. General illustration of address-point-based hybrid dasymetric technique used to determine residential population distribution. Each block group (A and B, represented by black squares) has an aggregated population of 12 people. Block group A contains 4 residential structures, which distributes 3 people to each house (12 / 4 = 3). Block group B contains 5 residential structures, which equates to 2.4 people per house. Converting the point data to raster pixels (represented with dashed lines) sums resident population per household in areas of higher housing density.

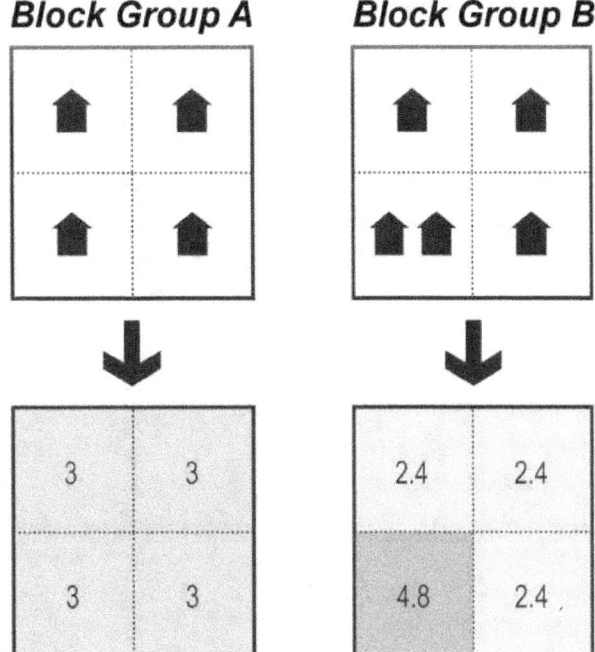

Figure 7. Maps of residential population at a 30-meter pixel resolution. *A*, Welches and surrounding unincorporated area, and *B*, Government Camp, Clackamas County, Oregon.

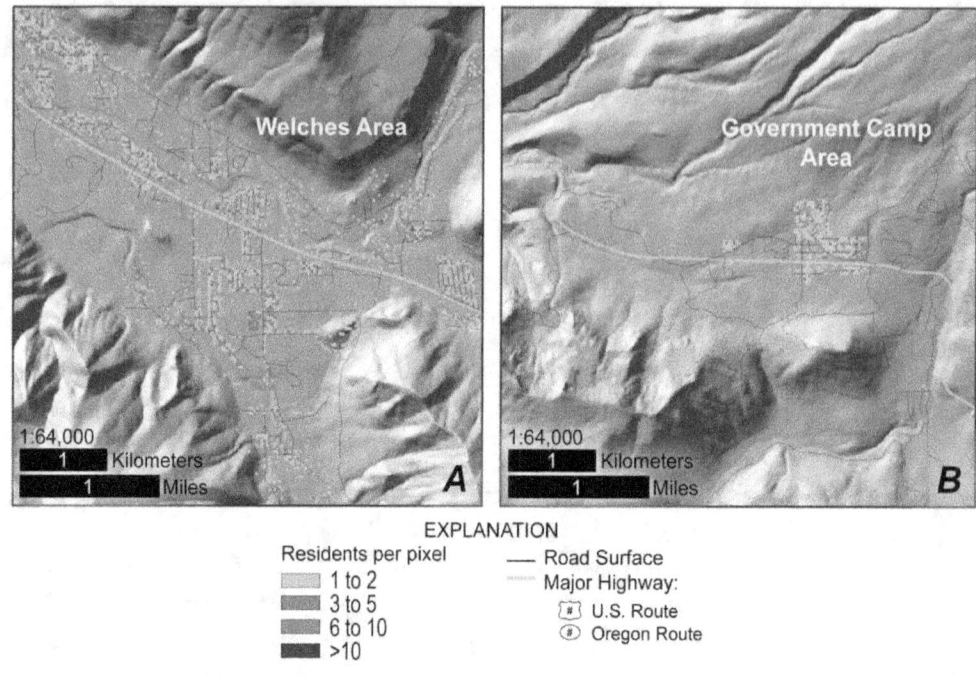

Figure 8. Three hundred-meter pixel resolution density maps of: *A*, residents by area, and *B*, employees by area, Clackamas County, Oregon.

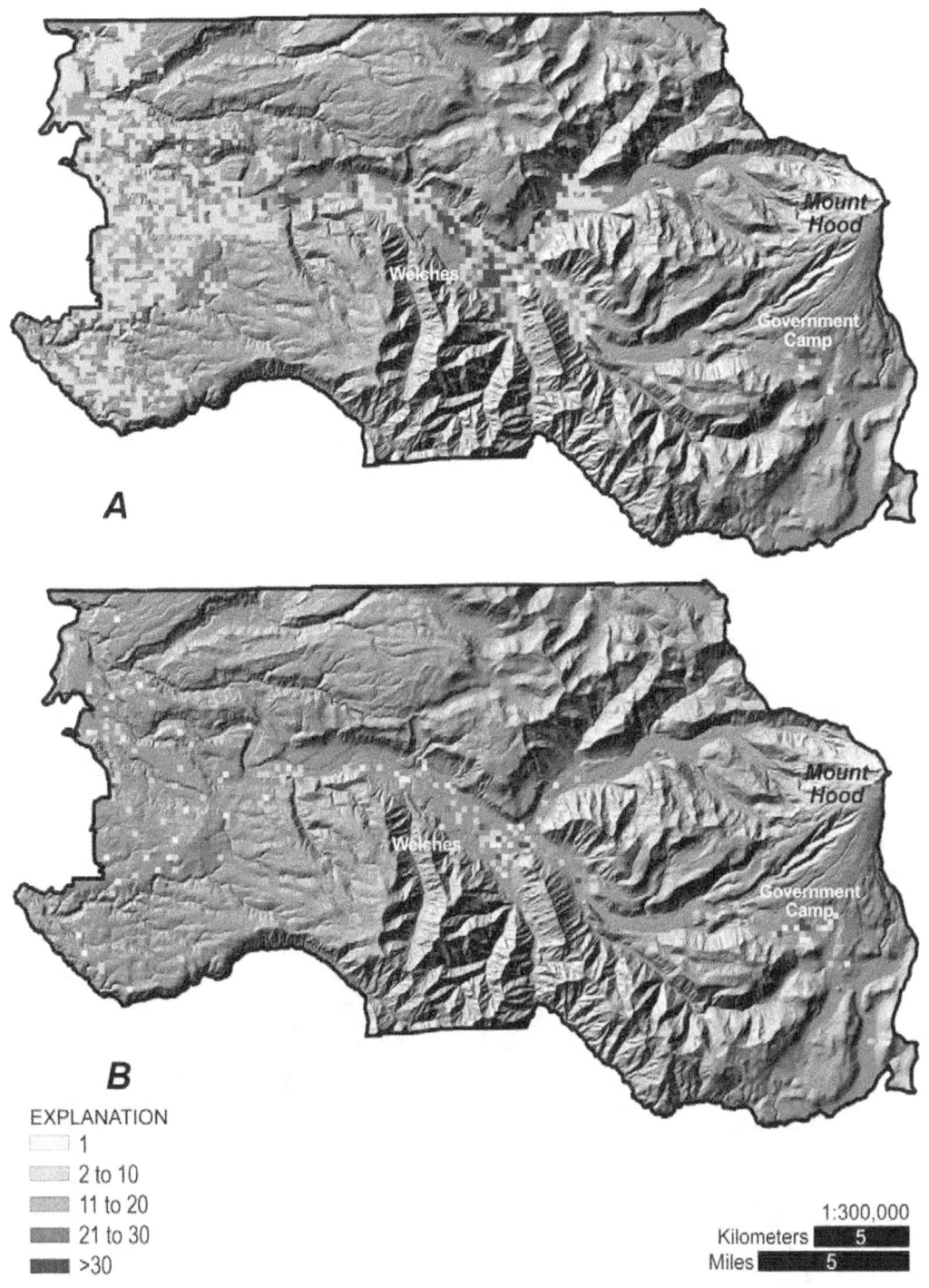

EXPLANATION
- 1
- 2 to 10
- 11 to 20
- 21 to 30
- >30

1:300,000
Kilometers 5
Miles 5

Figure 9. Three hundred-meter pixel resolution density maps of summer season attendance elements: *A*, daytime visitors to recreation sites and resident dependents by area, and *B*, overnight visitors by area, Clackamas County, Oregon.

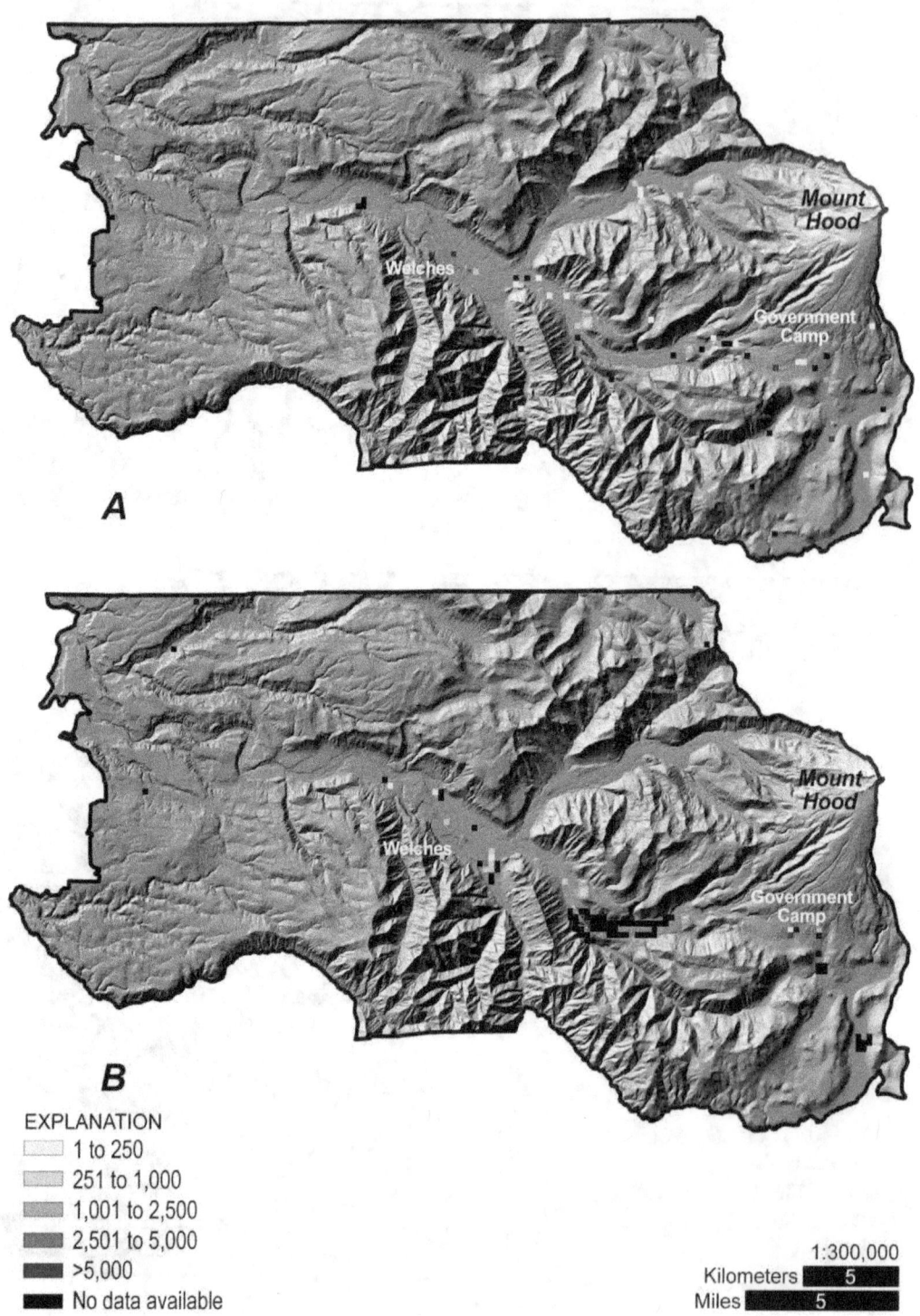

EXPLANATION
- 1 to 250
- 251 to 1,000
- 1,001 to 2,500
- 2,501 to 5,000
- >5,000
- No data available

1:300,000
Kilometers 5
Miles 5

Figure 10. Daily vehicle counts from Oregon Department of Transportation permanent recorder station located along U.S. Highway 26 east of Zigzag and west of Government Camp, Clackamas County, Oregon. *A*, daily maximum number of vehicles within any given hour, *B*, total daily count of vehicles, *C*, difference between east- and westbound traffic count of daily maximum, and *D*, difference between east- and westbound traffic count of daily total. No data were recorded in January or on isolated days in October and November.

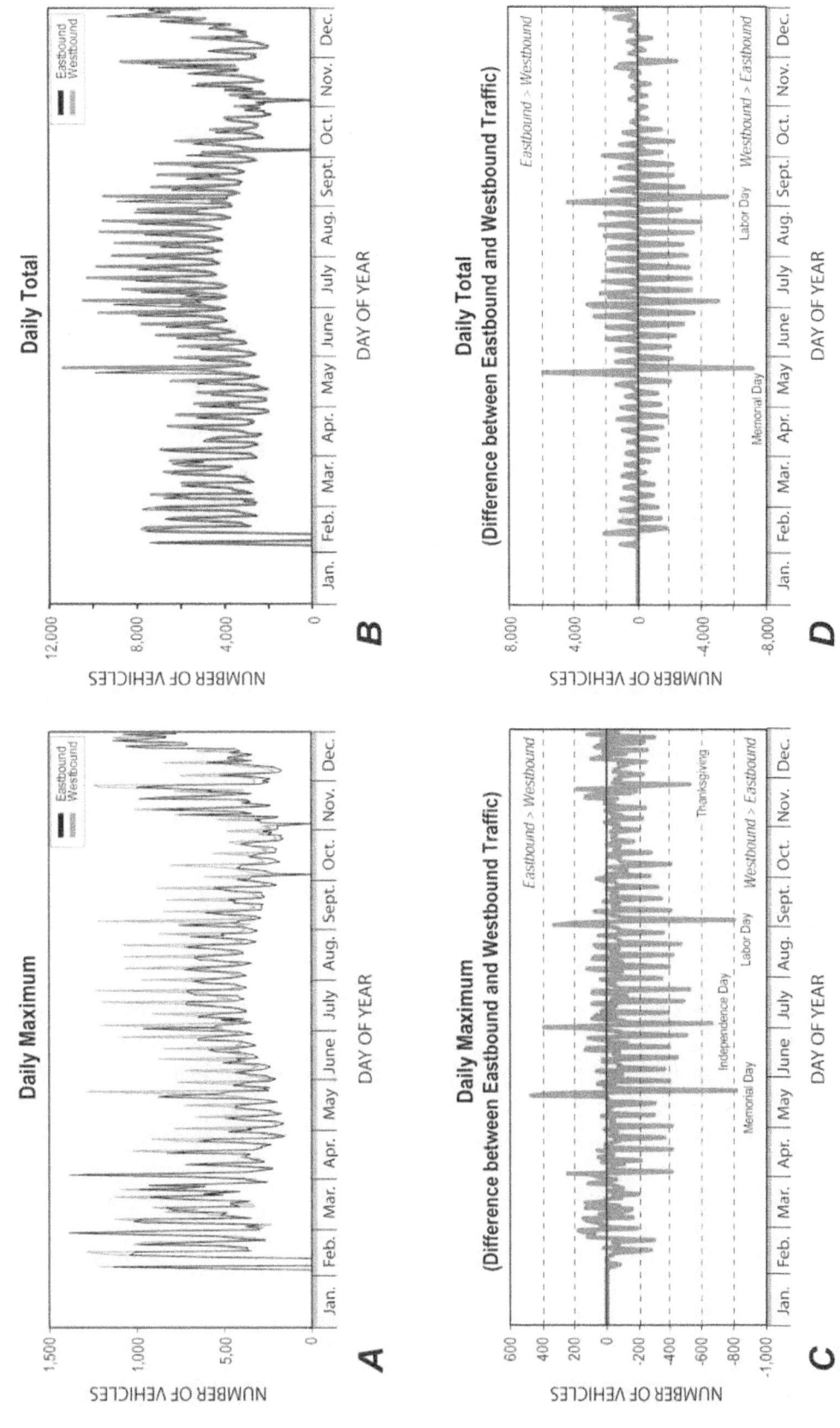

Figure 11. Map of 100-year and 500-year Federal Emergency Management Agency Flood Hazard Zones for the study area, Clackamas County, Oregon. Rivers mentioned in the report are labeled.

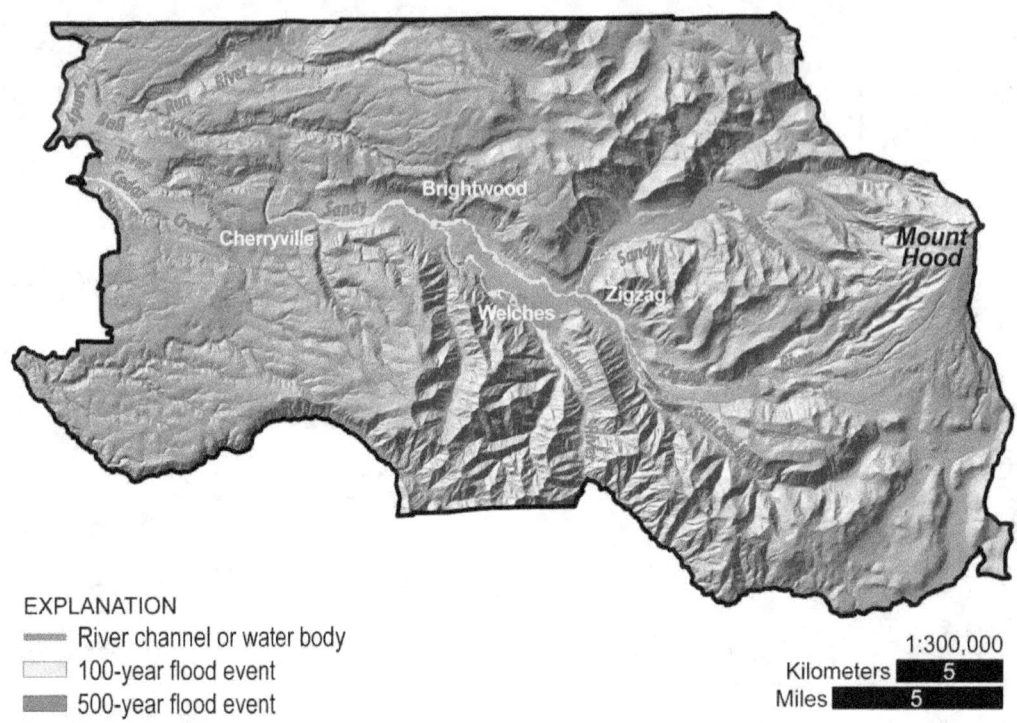

EXPLANATION
River channel or water body
100-year flood event
500-year flood event

1:300,000

Figure 12. Flood hazard exposure among *A*, study area homes and *B*, businesses, Clackamas County, Oregon. Values for a 500-year event are read as additions to the exposure calculated for a 100-year flood. Calculations are based on a total of 5,711 homes and 323 businesses; counts corresponding to listed percentages are in parentheses.

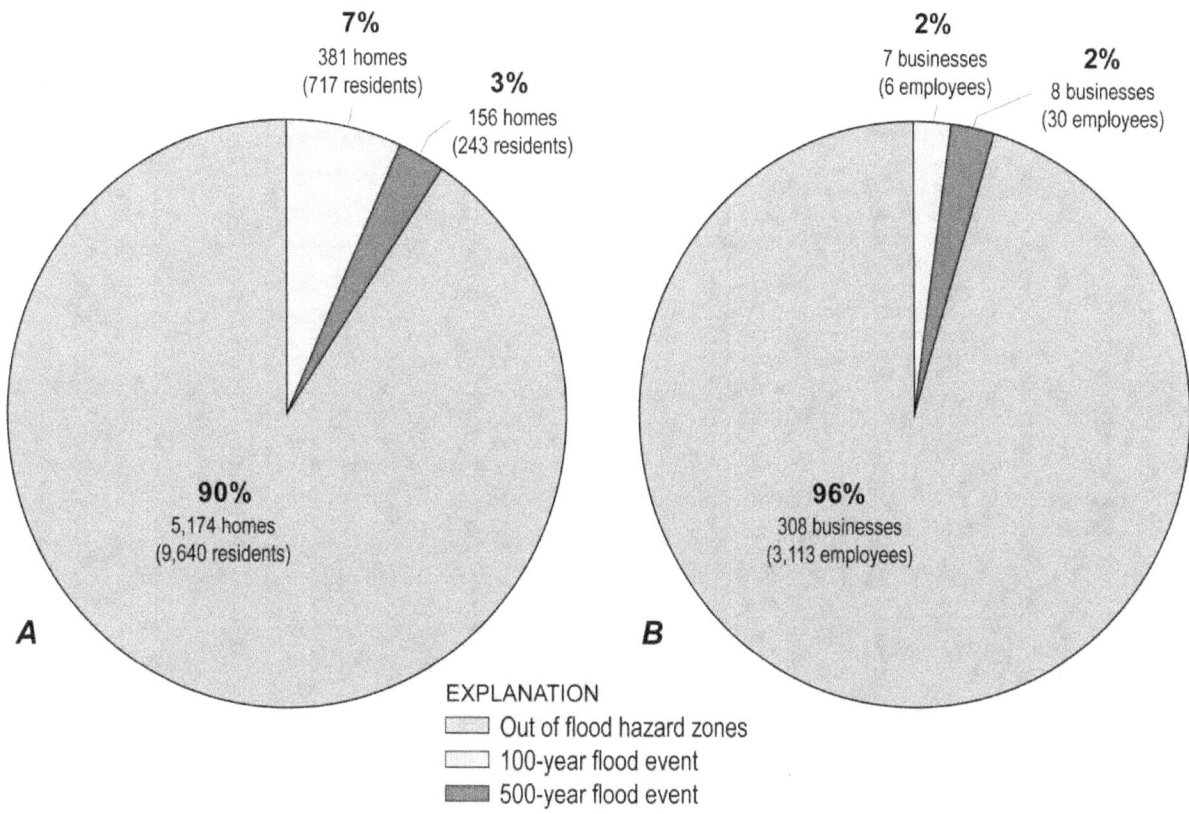

7%
381 homes
(717 residents)

3%
156 homes
(243 residents)

90%
5,174 homes
(9,640 residents)

A

2%
7 businesses
(6 employees)

2%
8 businesses
(30 employees)

96%
308 businesses
(3,113 employees)

B

EXPLANATION
Out of flood hazard zones
100-year flood event
500-year flood event

Figure 13. Flooding hazard exposure to employees by business sector, Clackamas County, Oregon. Values for a 500-year event are read as additions to the exposure calculated for a 100-year flood.

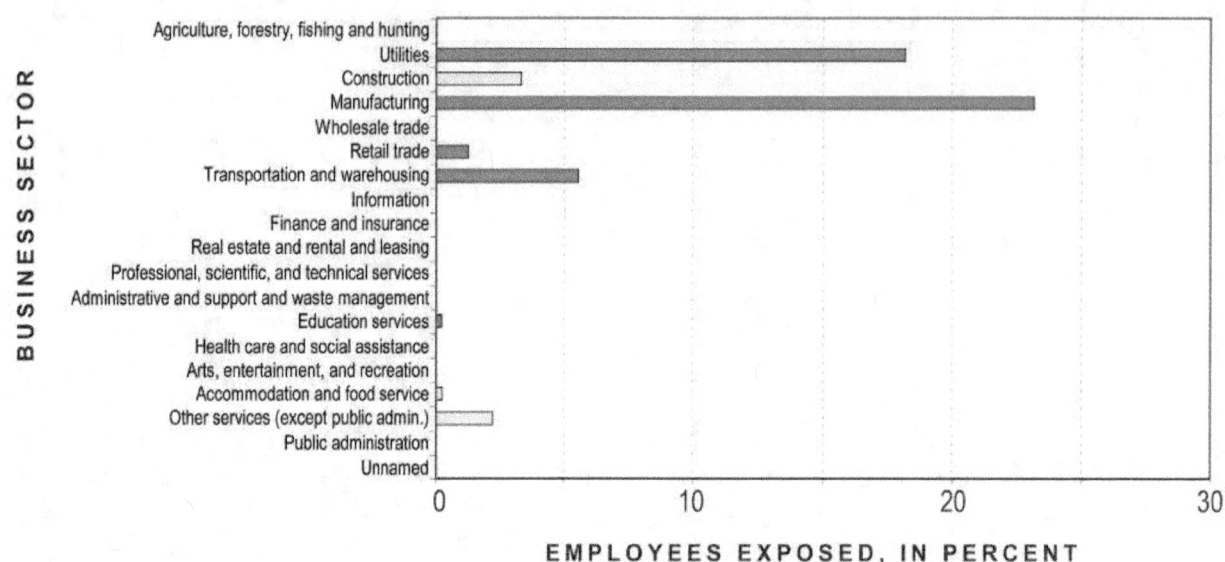

Figure 14. Map of overall wildfire risk to the study region as perceived by Clackamas County (Clackamas County, Oregon, 2005).

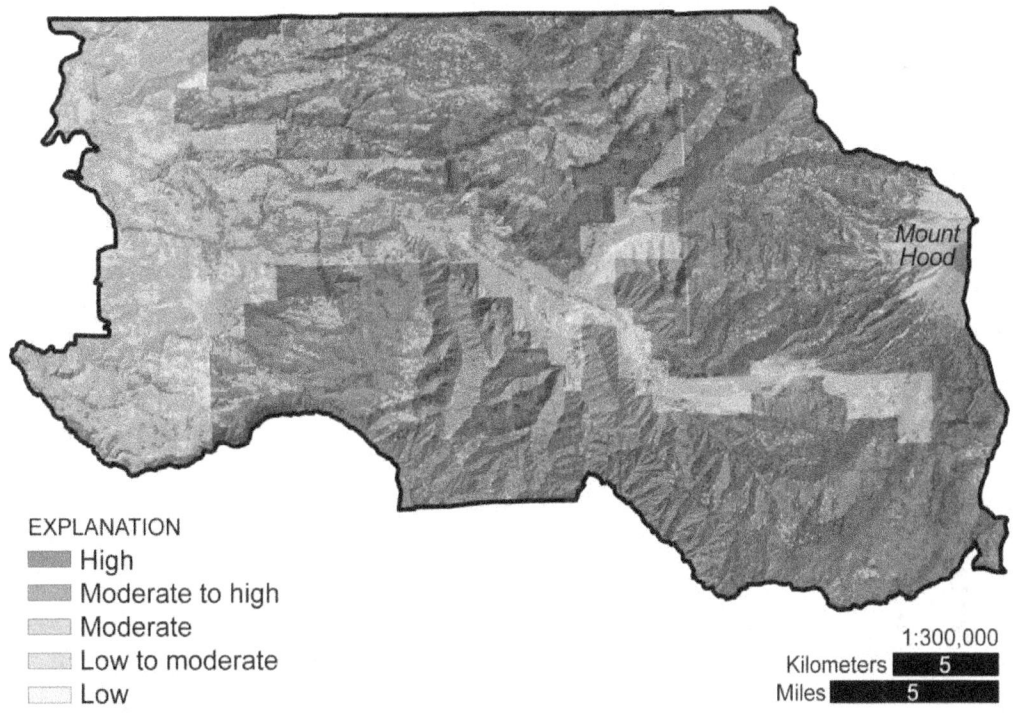

EXPLANATION
High
Moderate to high
Moderate
Low to moderate
Low

1:300,000
Kilometers 5
Miles 5

Figure 15. Wildfire-hazard risk within the study area, Clackamas County, Oregon. *A*, total area; *B*, among homes; *C*, among businesses; and *D*, among employees. Percentages are based on 5,711 homes and 323 businesses in the study area. The number of homes and businesses in each category are in parentheses.

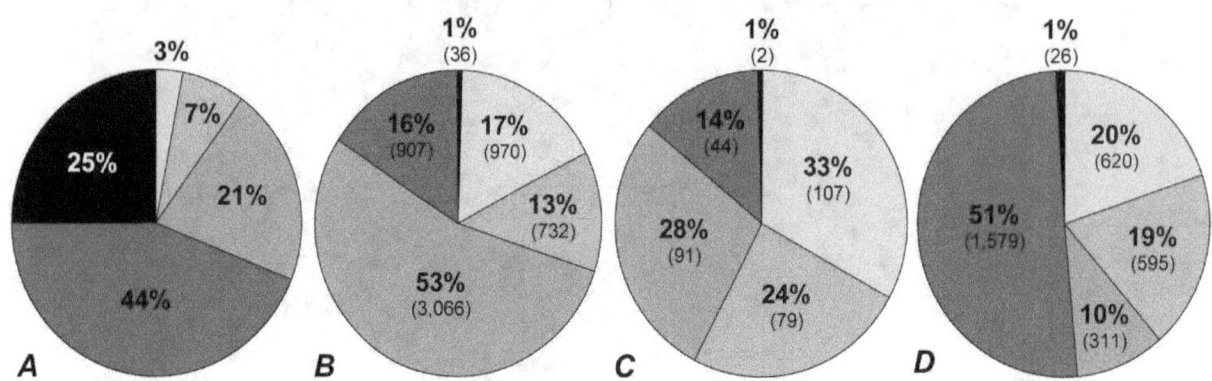

EXPLANATION
Wildfire risk zones
High
Moderate to high
Moderate
Low to moderate
Low

Figure 16. Wildfire-hazard risk to employees by business sector, Clackamas County, Oregon.

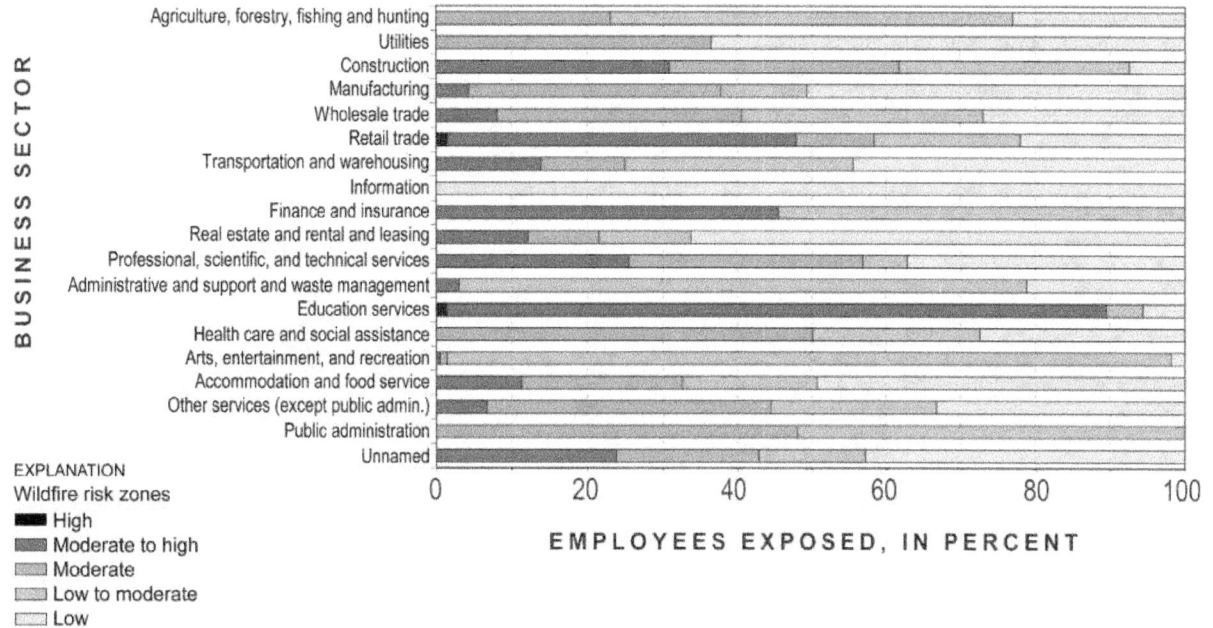

Figure 17. Wildfire-hazard risk among seasonal population groups, Clackamas County, Oregon. *A*, average monthly attendance by season, among resident dependents, at educational facilities; *B*, average monthly attendance by season, among overnight visitors, at lodging accommodations; and *C*, average monthly attendance by season, among residents and tourists, at day-use recreational areas and facilities. Daily attendance numbers are essentially equivalent to the monthly values in chart *A*, but are estimated in charts *B* and *C* by dividing seasonal monthly averages by 30.

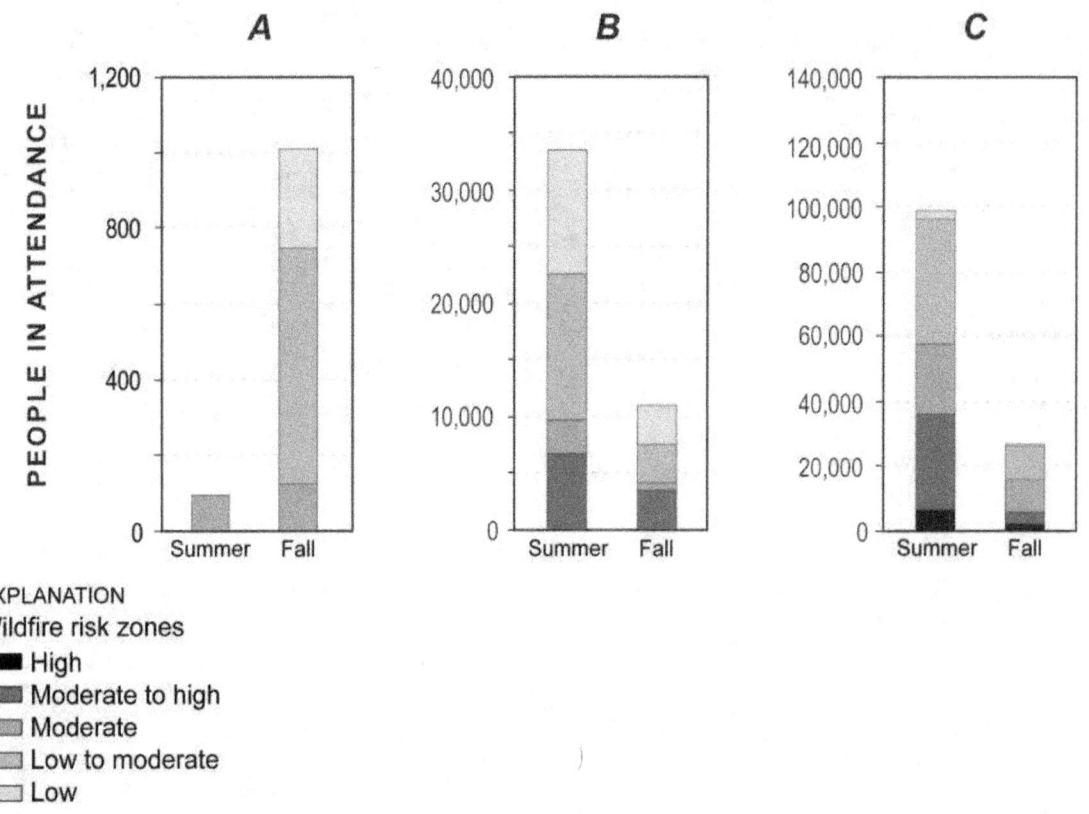

EXPLANATION
Wildfire risk zones
- ■ High
- ▨ Moderate to high
- ▨ Moderate
- ▨ Low to moderate
- ▨ Low

Figure 18. Map of volcano hazard zones for the study region (derived from Scott and others, 1997b), Clackamas County, Oregon. Three different hazard zone types are noted: (1) a proximal hazard zone, (2) a distal lahar hazard zone for a typical eruption event, and (3) an extended distal lahar hazard zone for a worst-case scenario event. Crater Rock, the remnant of a previously erupted lava dome and an area of active volcanic fumaroles, is labeled on Mount Hood.

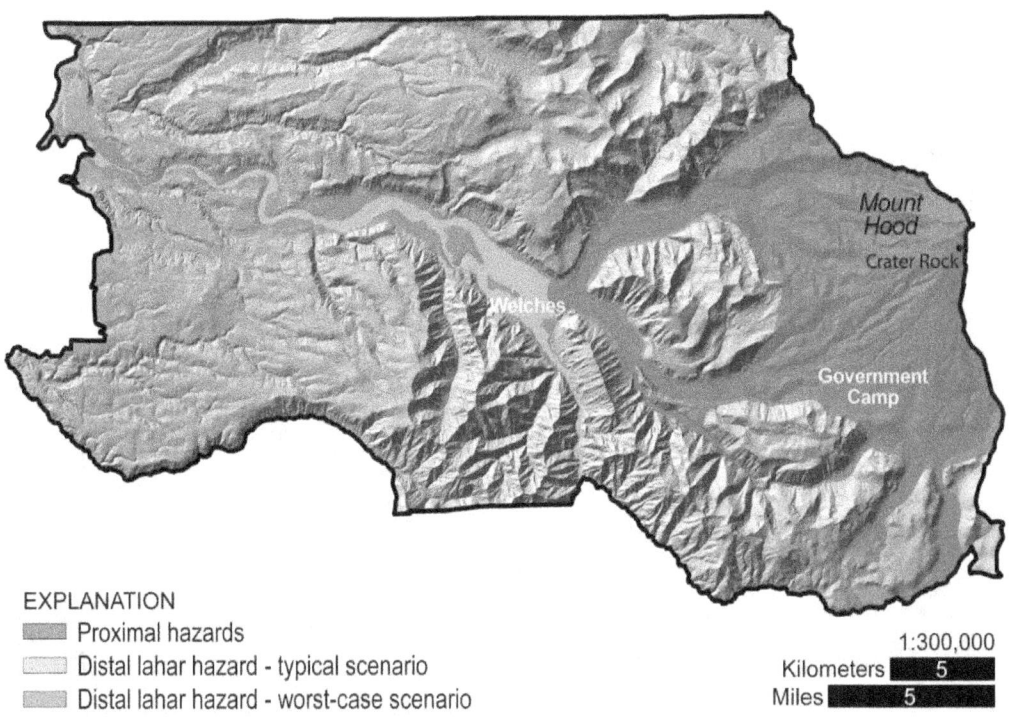

EXPLANATION

▨ Proximal hazards
▨ Distal lahar hazard - typical scenario
▨ Distal lahar hazard - worst-case scenario

1:300,000
Kilometers ▬▬ 5
Miles ▬▬ 5

Figure 19. Effect of Mount Hood's topographic profile on potential distance traveled by a pyroclastic flow and ash-cloud surge (modified from Brantley and Scott, 1993), Clackamas County, Oregon. Diagram depicts a hypothetical maximum flow generated by collapse of a substantial lava dome at Crater Rock. A flow of this size would take less than 30 minutes to reach its maximum extent. However, such an event likely would be preceded by indicators of volcanic unrest that would be detected by U.S. Geological Survey monitoring (William Scott, oral communication, June 2012.

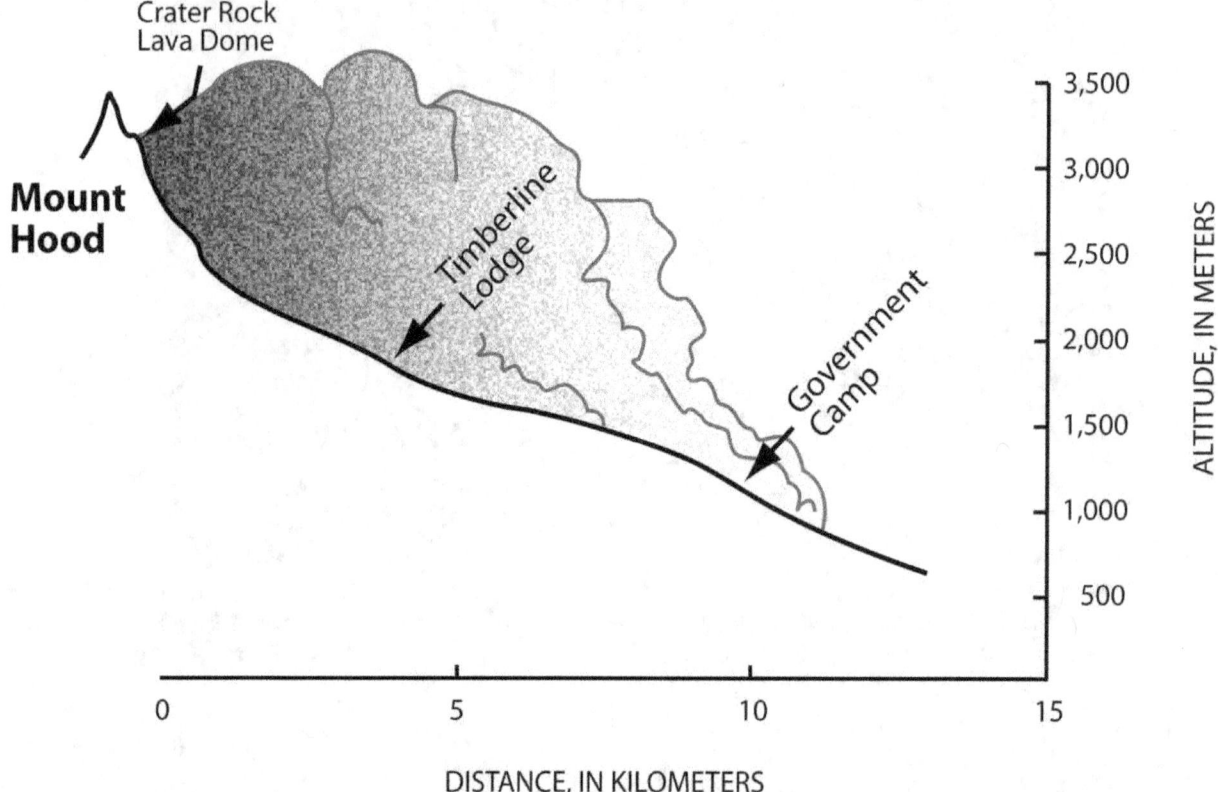

Figure 20. Volcano hazard exposure among *A*, homes, *B*, businesses, and *C*, employees, in the study area, Clackamas County, Oregon. Values for a worst-case scenario lahar event are read as additions to the exposure calculated for a typical event. Calculations are based on a total of 5,711 homes, 323 businesses, and 3,149 employees.

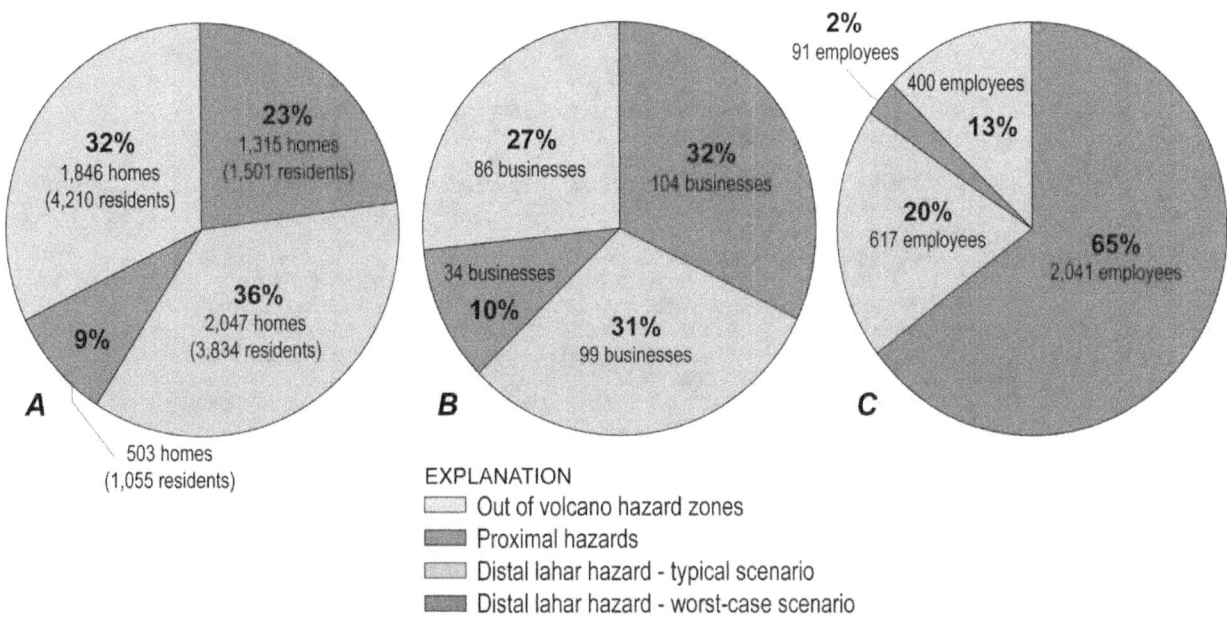

EXPLANATION
- Out of volcano hazard zones
- Proximal hazards
- Distal lahar hazard - typical scenario
- Distal lahar hazard - worst-case scenario

Figure 21. Volcano hazard exposure to employees by business sector, Clackasmas County, Oregon. Presented are two types of hazard categories (proximal and distal) and two levels of events (typical eruption and worst-case scenario) influencing the distal hazards; values for a worst-case scenario lahar event are read as additions to the exposure calculated for a typical event.

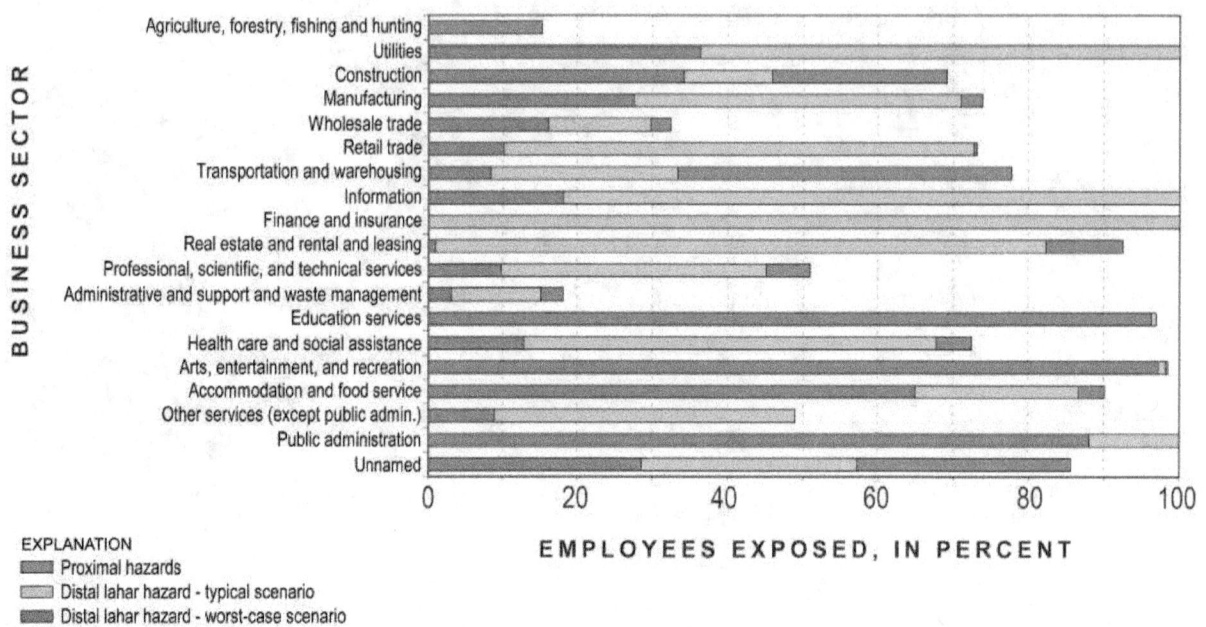

Figure 22. Volcano-hazard exposure among seasonal population groups, Clackamas County, Oregon. *A*, average monthly attendance by season, among resident dependents, at educational facilities; *B*, average monthly attendance by season, among overnight visitors, at lodging accommodations; and *C*, average monthly attendance by season, among residents and tourists, at day-use recreational areas and facilities. Daily attendance numbers in chart *A* are essentially equivalent to the monthly values, but can be estimated in charts *B* and *C* by dividing seasonal monthly averages by 30. Proximal-hazard exposure remains the same regardless of event magnitude, and the difference in population exposure between event magnitudes among distal hazards is generally negligible.

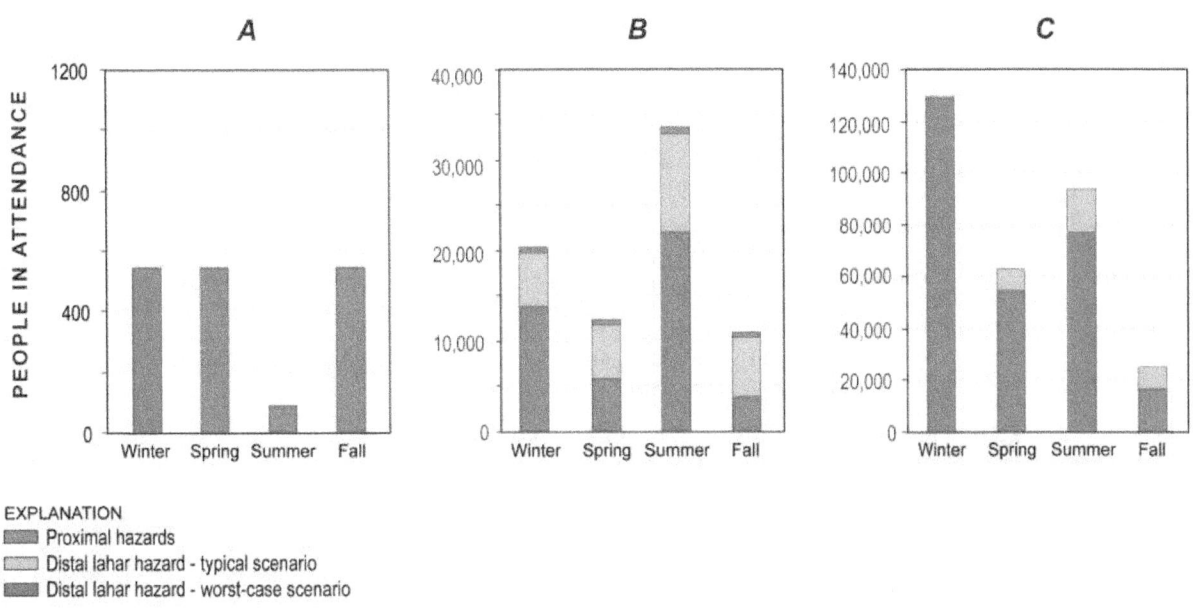

EXPLANATION
- Proximal hazards
- Distal lahar hazard - typical scenario
- Distal lahar hazard - worst-case scenario

Appendix A

The North American Classification System (NAICS) is used to categorize economic activity in Canada, Mexico, and the United States. Of the entire eight-digit code used by NAICS, the first two digits denote a business sector. The following chart provides descriptions for each business sector recognized within this study.

Sector number	Description
11	Agriculture, forestry, fishing, and hunting
22	Utilities
23	Construction
31-33	Manufacturing
42	Wholesale trade
44-45	Retail trade
48-49	Transportation and warehousing
51	Information
52	Finance and insurance
53	Real estate and rental and leasing
54	Professional, scientific, and technical services
56	Administrative and support and waste management and remediation services
61	Education services
61	Health care and social assistance
71	Arts, entertainment, and recreation
72	Accommodation and food services
81	Other services (except public administration)
92	Public administration

Appendix B

Master data table of hazard exposure among resident and employee population groups, Clackamas County, Oregon.

Hazard Exposure		Households		Residents		Businesses		Employees		Sales Volume	
		#	%	#	%	#	%	#	%	#	%
Study Area Total		5,711	100	10,600	100	323	100	3,149	100	$361,296,000	100
Flood	100-year	381	7	717	7	7	2	6	<1	$1,408,000	<1
	500-year	537	10	960	9	15	4	36	1	$18,771,000	5
Wildfire	High	36	1	74	1	2	1	26	1	$4,464,000	1
	Moderate-to-high	907	16	1,846	17	44	14	1,597	51	$115,692,000	32
	Moderate	3,066	53	5,742	54	91	28	311	10	$63,398,000	18
	Low-to-moderate	732	13	1,449	14	79	24	595	19	$97,705,000	27
	Low	970	17	1,489	14	107	33	620	20	$80,037,000	22
Volcano	Proximal hazards	1,315	23	1,501	14	104	32	2,041	65	$166,533,000	46
	Distal hazard (typical scenario)	2,047	36	3,834	36	99	31	617	20	$87,907,000	24
	Distal hazard (worst-case scenario)	2,550	45	4,889	46	133	41	708	22	$100,300,000	28
	Total hazards (typical scenario)	3,362	59	5,335	50	203	63	2,658	84	$254,440,000	70
	Total hazards (worst-case scenario)	3,865	68	6,390	60	237	73	2,749	87	$266,833,000	74

Appendix C

Master data table of hazard exposure among service populations, Clackamas County, Oregon.

Hazard Exposure		Winter	Spring	Summer	Fall
		Resident dependents at educational facilities			
Wildfire	High	0	0	0	0
	Moderate-to-high	0	0	0	0
	Moderate	123	123	93	123
	Low-to-moderate	623	623	0	623
	Low	266	266	0	266
	Grand total	1,012	1,012	93	1,012
Volcano	Proximal hazards	549	549	93	549
	Distal hazard (typical)	0	0	0	0
	Distal hazard (worst-case)	0	0	0	0
	Grand total (typical)	549	549	93	549
	Grand total (worst-case)	549	549	93	549
		Overnight visitors			
Wildfire	High	15	1	80	1
	Moderate-to-high	6,882	4,783	6,677	3,456
	Moderate	1,313	1,065	2,908	676
	Low-to-moderate	6,493	3,205	12,918	3,336
	Low	5,673	3,303	10,982	3,525
	Grand total	20,376	12,357	33,565	10,994
Volcano	Proximal hazards	13,912	5,844	21,992	3,807
	Distal hazard (typical)	5,918	6,045	10,750	6,589
	Distal hazard (worst-case)	6,464	6,513	11,573	7,187
	Grand total (typical)	19,830	11,889	32,742	10,396
	Grand total (worst-case)	20,376	12,357	33,565	10,994
		Daytime visitors to recreation sites			
Wildfire	High	0	94	6,770	2,281
	Moderate-to-high	49,658	32,434	29,264	3,626
	Moderate	0	9,205	21,529	9,894
	Low-to-moderate	78,905	21,616	38,520	10,041
	Low	700	617	2,635	742
	Grand total	129,263	63,966	98,718	26,584
Volcano	Proximal hazards	128,813	54,664	76,809	17,068
	Distal hazard (typical)	450	8,188	17,057	8,286
	Distal hazard (worst-case)	450	8,200	17,107	8,318
	Grand total (typical)	129,263	62,852	93,866	25,354
	Grand total (worst-case)	129,263	62,864	93,916	25,386

www.ingramcontent.com/pod-product-compliance
Lightning Source LLC
Chambersburg PA
CBHW080450290526
45791CB00008BA/2666